NEW DIRECTIONS FOR TEACHING AND LEARNING

Robert J. Menges, *Northwestern University*
EDITOR-IN-CHIEF

Marilla D. Svinicki, *University of Texas, Austin*
ASSOCIATE EDITOR

Understanding Self-Regulated Learning

Paul R. Pintrich
University of Michigan

EDITOR

Number 63, Fall 1995

JOSSEY-BASS PUBLISHERS
San Francisco

UNDERSTANDING SELF-REGULATED LEARNING
Paul R. Pintrich (ed.)
New Directions for Teaching and Learning, no. 63
Robert J. Menges, Editor-in-Chief
Marilla D. Svinicki, Associate Editor

august 28, 1995

Microfilm copies of issues and articles are available in 16mm and 35mm, as well as microfiche in 105mm, through University Microfilms Inc., 300 North Zeeb Road, Ann Arbor, Michigan 48106-1346.

LC 85-644763   ISSN 0271-0633   ISBN 0-7879-9978-4

NEW DIRECTIONS FOR TEACHING AND LEARNING is part of The Jossey-Bass Higher and Adult Education Series and is published quarterly by Jossey-Bass Inc., Publishers, 350 Sansome Street, San Francisco, California 94104-1342. Second-class postage paid at San Francisco, California, and at additional mailing offices. POSTMASTER: Send address changes to New Directions for Teaching and Learning, Jossey-Bass Inc., Publishers, 350 Sansome Street, San Francisco, California 94104-1342.

SUBSCRIPTIONS for 1995 cost $48.00 for individuals and $64.00 for institutions, agencies, and libraries.

EDITORIAL CORRESPONDENCE should be sent to the editor-in-chief, Robert J. Menges, Northwestern University, Center for the Teaching Professions, 2003 Sheridan Road, Evanston, Illinois 60208-2610.

Cover photograph by Richard Blair/Color & Light © 1990.

TCF Manufactured in the United States of America on Lyons Falls Pathfinder Tradebook. This paper is acid-free and 100 percent totally chlorine-free.

CONTENTS

From the Series Editors

About This Publication. Since 1980, *New Directions for Teaching and Learning* (NDTL) has brought a unique blend of theory, research, and practice to leaders in postsecondary education. NDTL sourcebooks strive not only for solid substance but also for timeliness, compactness, and accessibility.

The series has four goals: to inform readers about current and future directions in teaching and learning in postsecondary education, to illuminate the context that shapes these new directions, to illustrate these new directions through examples from real settings, and to propose ways in which these new directions can be incorporated into still other settings.

This publication reflects our view that teaching deserves respect as a high form of scholarship. We believe that significant scholarship is conducted not only by researchers who report results of empirical investigations but also by practitioners who share disciplined reflections about teaching. Contributors to NDTL approach questions of teaching and learning as seriously as they approach substantive questions in their own disciplines, and they deal not only with pedagogical issues but also with the intellectual and social context in which these issues arise. Authors deal on the one hand with theory and research and on the other with practice, and they translate from research and theory to practice and back again.

About This Volume. In this volume, a distinguished group of researchers and teachers introduces us to an emerging area of scholarship that holds singular importance for postsecondary education: the capacity of students to regulate their own learning. This work gives faculty a new way to think about teaching and learning and a set of strategies that can enhance students' self-regulation. It is difficult to imagine a topic more pertinent to equipping students not only to succeed in college but also to flourish as lifelong learners.

Robert J. Menges, *Editor-in-Chief*
Marilla D. Svinicki, *Associate Editor*

ROBERT J. MENGES, *editor-in-chief, is professor of education and social policy at Northwestern University, and senior researcher, National Center on Post-secondary Teaching, Learning, and Assessment.*

MARILLA D. SVINICKI, *associate editor, is director of the Center for Teaching Effectiveness, University of Texas at Austin.*

EDITOR'S NOTES

Self-regulated learning is a fairly new construct in research on student performance and achievement in classroom settings, and it is important for all educators, including college faculty. Research on self-regulated learning that has focused on K-12 students is now being supplemented by research with college students and has significant implications for both students and faculty. The purpose of this volume is to provide a sampling of some of the central issues in self-regulated learning in college courses and classrooms.

First, as in any relatively new construct in psychology, there are issues concerning the definition and role of the construct. The chapters by Pintrich, Zimmerman and Paulsen, and Garcia all address how self-regulated learning can be defined in the context of the college classroom. A second issue of importance to college students and faculty concerns how self-regulated learning can be fostered in college courses and classrooms. All the chapters in the volume address this issue to some extent, but the ones by Hagen and Weinstein and by Trawick and Corno discuss it most directly. Finally, college faculty are often interested in how they can use ideas as "tools" to think about their own classrooms. The construct of self-regulated learning can be seen as an intellectual tool that helps faculty think differently about their role as instructors. The chapters by Karabenick and Collins-Eaglin and by Coppola describe how different faculty have used the research on self-regulated learning in a variety of ways in their own classrooms.

All of the chapters in this volume reflect current research and thinking about self-regulated learning for college students. Much more research and development is needed on this important area of research, but these chapters help to provide a context for our efforts to improve college learning and teaching.

Paul R. Pintrich
Editor

PAUL R. PINTRICH is associate professor in the Combined Program in Education and Psychology at the University of Michigan, Ann Arbor.

Self-regulated learning is an important component of learning for college students. Students can learn how to become self-regulated learners, and faculty can foster self-regulated learning in their classrooms.

Understanding Self-Regulated Learning

Paul R. Pintrich

This volume of *New Directions for Teaching and Learning* focuses on self-regulated learning for college students. The term *self-regulated learning* refers to a fairly new construct in research on college student learning, but it has very important implications for both students and faculty. The chapters in this volume provide an overview of current research on self-regulated learning as it applies to postsecondary education. My goal in this chapter is to introduce and define the construct of self-regulated learning. In addition, I discuss why self-regulated learning is important to college students and faculty and what can be done to improve self-regulated learning. In this way, I foreshadow many of the issues addressed in the following chapters, thereby providing an organizational framework for the reader.

What Is Self-Regulated Learning?

The term *self-regulated learning* may sound somewhat foreign to many readers' ears, but most faculty members recognize a self-regulated learner when they encounter one in a class. The following examples describe both students who are good self-regulating learners and students who have difficulties regulating their own learning. I think that after looking at these examples most readers will recall their own experiences with the two types of learners.

    Tom, Who Keeps Up with Assignments. Tom is a first-year student at a community college. He also works part-time to help pay for his tuition. He is very organized and uses a schedule book to keep track of his work and course schedule. He may miss class occasionally because he was working late the night before, but he always gets the notes from other students and talks to the faculty member about what he missed in class. He keeps track of his course assignments in his notebooks and always turns in his work on time. His grades will be good enough to allow him to transfer to a four-year university when he finishes his two-year program.

Lynda, Whose Attention Wanders. Lynda is a junior psychology major at a major research university. She loves to read about psychology and fantasize about what it will be like when she is a psychologist working with children with emotional problems. Often, when she is reading psychology, and even more when studying subjects she is less interested in, she reads the words in the text but does not seem to monitor her understanding. Sometimes, she gets to the end of the chapter and does not even realize that she was daydreaming while she was reading. Other times, she does realize that she was not paying much attention to what she was reading, but she has so much other work to do that she does not go back and reread the text. She figures she will review the material before the test but often does not find the time. She gets average grades, which leaves her a little puzzled since she does spend two to three hours a night reading and studying for her classes.

Michael, Who Doubts His Ability. Michael is a freshman at a large comprehensive university. He is thinking about becoming a medical doctor and is taking a number of courses for a premed major, such as biology, chemistry, and calculus. He did very well in high school, especially in his science courses, although he often got very nervous before tests. In college, he is confronted with many other good students in his premed classes. He often feels as though he cannot do the work at the same level as they do. Doubts about his ability to do well lead him to study more, but his problem with anxiety during tests gets even worse. He spends many hours trying to memorize the course material, but on exams, it seems that his mind will go blank. He then starts to worry about flunking out of premed and disappointing his parents. His performance on tests is generally poor, although he does very well on his homework assignments and labs.

Dianne, Who Plans Ahead. Dianne is a senior at a small liberal arts college. She is usually one of the most involved students in class. She pays attention and is not afraid to ask questions when she does not understand something, even if the questions might seem rather basic. She reads course material carefully, making notes, charts, and diagrams of what she is reading. She often makes notes to herself while reading to ask the teacher about something in the textbook that does not coincide with what the teacher lectured on the previous day. Before a test, she figures out what kind of test it will be (multiple-choice or essay) and adjusts her studying to fit the test. For multiple-choice tests, she concentrates on knowing the terms and concepts. She integrates her lecture notes and readings to make sure she knows all the important concepts. For essay tests, she does not spend as much time memorizing terms and concepts. She makes outlines, focusing on how the material fits together and what are the "big" theories or themes in the course material. She tries to predict what types of essay questions will be on the test and makes up a short outline of how she might answer each question. Needless to say, she does very well in all her classes.

Characteristics of Self-Regulated Learning. These four students all represent different aspects of successful and unsuccessful self-regulation of learning. It seems clear that Dianne and Tom are the successful self-regulated learners, while Lynda and Michael have some difficulties in regulating their learning. These four students also represent how students may regulate three different dimensions of their learning: their observable *behavior,* their *motivation and affect,* and their *cognition.*

There are three characteristics, or components, of self-regulated learning that function in relation to these three dimensions. First, self-regulated learners attempt to *control* their behavior, motivation and affect, and cognition. A good analogy is a thermostat that regulates room temperature by monitoring the current temperature and then turning on or off the heating/cooling unit to bring the actual temperature in line with the preset desired temperature. In the same way, students can monitor their own behavior, motivation, and cognition, and then regulate and adjust these characteristics to fit the demands of the situation. The second important component of self-regulated learning, also suggested by the thermostat analogy, is that there is some *goal* the student is attempting to accomplish, analogous to a preset desired temperature. This goal provides the standard by which the student can monitor and judge her own performance and then make the appropriate adjustments. The third important characteristic of self-regulated learning is that *the individual student*—not someone else like a parent or teacher—must be in control of his actions, hence the "self" prefix in the term self-regulated learning. For example, students might change their behavior in a classroom, but this would not be considered self-regulation if it is only in response to a requirement by the teacher, and if once the requirement is removed, they no longer engage in the behavior. In short, self-regulated learning involves the active, goal-directed, self-control of behavior, motivation, and cognition for academic tasks by an individual student.

Further Examples of Self-Regulated Learning. Applying this definition of self-regulated learning to the four students I have just described, we can see how they vary in their self-regulation. Tom, the community college student, is regulating his behavior by keeping a schedule of his commitments and keeping track of his school assignments. His goal is to do well enough at the community college so he can transfer to a four-year school, and his organization and management of his time and work schedules seems to be facilitating this goal. In contrast, if Tom were engaging in this behavior as a requirement for his courses or from his advisor, he would not be self-regulating his own behavior. His behavior would be regulated but by others, not by him.

Lynda is having difficulties monitoring and regulating her cognition. In particular, when she daydreams without realizing that she is not paying attention to her reading, she is having difficulty monitoring her cognition. She does not seem to be aware of these lapses in her attention and cognition. Moreover, because she does not seem to be aware of her problem, she does not take the next step of regulating her cognition, of going back and rereading the text she missed while she was daydreaming. All students sometimes daydream and lose attention when reading text material. The important difference between a self-regulated learner and other students is that a self-regulated learner will become aware of her loss of attention and comprehension and go back and repair her deficiency by rereading the material. In addition, there may be occasions when students actually do pay attention during their reading but still do not understand the material very well. A self-regulated learner will test her comprehension by asking herself questions about what she just read, and then, if her comprehension is not adequate, will take steps, such as rereading, to improve that comprehension. Barry Zimmerman and Andrew Paulsen discuss different aspects of self-monitoring of behavior and cognition later in this volume.

It might also be noted that in Lynda's case, her goal of being a psychologist might be interfering with her learning because it seems to be the starting point for her daydreams. Accordingly, Lynda may have to change her goals when she is studying, to make them short-term and proximal and appropriate to the task (for example, "My goal tonight is to read a chapter in my textbook and understand it"), rather than focusing only on her more distal and global goals such as becoming a psychologist. When individuals regulate their goals to fit a specific task, it is a type of self-regulation of both cognition and motivation. In Chapter Two, Zimmerman and Paulsen point out how self-monitoring of learning can depend on the types of goals students have when they approach academic tasks.

Michael is a classic case of a student who is having difficulty regulating his motivation and affect for schoolwork. Although he seems to have the general knowledge and skills to succeed in college given his high school performance, he seems to doubt his ability to succeed in college. Such self-doubt about competence is referred to as a lack of *self-efficacy*. Students who are high in self-efficacy are confident in their skills and abilities to do well in school, and usually they actually do well and engage in appropriate use of cognitive learning strategies (Pintrich and De Groot, 1990). In addition, Michael's lack of self-efficacy is coupled with debilitating affect in the form of high test anxiety, a normal occurrence when self-efficacy is low (Bandura, 1986). Finally, Michael's high level of anxiety seems to lead him to use simple memorization cognitive strategies, rather than other, deeper processing strategies for learning. Nevertheless, there are ways in which the negative affect of test anxiety can be regulated and controlled by the learner (Bandura, 1986), as well as ways for students to regulate their self-efficacy (Schunk, 1994). One of the ways in which people can regulate self-efficacy is to make comparisons, not to other students but to their own performance, and to focus on mastery of the material rather than on competing with others. If Michael can concentrate on his own learning of the material and begin to see how his own effort can make a difference in his performance, his efficacy will improve, and he also may become less anxious about tests. There are other self-regulatory techniques a student can use to help manage test anxiety (see Covington, 1992). In Chapter Three, Teresa Garcia describes different ways college students may regulate their motivation, including their efficacy and anxiety, in the classroom and as they prepare for exams.

Finally, Dianne exemplifies an effective self-regulated learner, especially in terms of controlling her cognition. She monitors her comprehension of class lecture material and is not afraid to ask questions to improve her understanding. When reading, she uses various elaboration cognitive strategies such as outlining and taking notes, which should help her process the material in a deep and meaningful manner. She changes the way she studies in order to adapt to the test demands. She concentrates on memorizing terms and concepts when she has a multiple-choice exam. For essay tests, she uses cognitive learning strategies such as outlining and integration of course material, which should result in deeper processing of the material, better retention, and better performance than if she just concentrates on memorizing terms. In addition, given that she is not afraid to ask "dumb" questions, she is probably focused on mastery of the material, not just grades. A mastery goal orientation has been positively related to self-regulated learning in a number of studies (see Ames, 1992, for a review), in contrast to a performance goal orientation, which is focused on grades and besting others. Anastasia Hagen and Claire Ellen Weinstein discuss in Chapter Four the implications of these two goal orientations in college classrooms and the effect they can have on self-regulated learning.

In summary, self-regulated learning involves the regulation of three general aspects of academic learning. First, self-regulation of behavior involves the *active control of the various resources* students have available to them, such as their time, their study environment (for example, the place in which they study), and their use of others such as peers and faculty members to help them (Garcia and Pintrich, 1994; Pintrich, Smith, Garcia, and McKeachie, 1993). Second, self-regulation of motivation and affect involves *controlling and changing motivational beliefs* such as efficacy and goal orientation, so that students can adapt to the demands of a course. In addition, students can learn how to control their emotions and affect (such as anxiety) in ways that improve their learning. Third and finally, self-regulation of cognition involves the *control of various cognitive strategies for learning,* such as the use of deep processing strategies that result in better learning and performance than students showed previously (Garcia and Pintrich, 1994; Pintrich, Smith, Garcia, and McKeachie, 1993).

Importance of Self-Regulated Learning for College Students and Faculty

Given this definition and description of self-regulated learning, why is it of import for college students and faculty? Besides the obvious advantage for both students and faculty that self-regulating learners will be better students and learn more, the idea of self-regulated learning offers an optimistic perspective on college learning and teaching. This perspective includes several assumptions about learning and teaching that have important implications for students and faculty.

Students Can Learn to Be Self-Regulated. Self-regulated learning is a way of approaching academic tasks that students learn through experience and self-reflection. It is not a characteristic that is genetically based or formed early in life so that students are "stuck" with it for the rest of their lives. Models of self-regulated learning argue against the notion of intelligence as a characteristic that varies among students and is unchangeable after a certain point in life. There may be students who are more or less self-regulating over time and across different classes, but all students can learn how to be self-regulating, regardless of age, gender, ethnic background, actual ability level, prior knowledge, or motivation. This is a much more optimistic view of learning and our students than we once had, implying that all students can learn how to become self-regulated learners and that faculty can explicitly help them achieve this goal. In Chapter Five, LaVergne Trawick and Lyn Corno discuss a specific intervention to help "at-risk" students become more self-regulating.

Self-Regulated Learning Is Controllable. Related to the first assumption, this view proposes that self-regulated learning is a way to approach academic tasks that the individual student can control. Self-regulated learning is not a personality "style" or trait that the individual has no control over, as suggested, for example, by the Myers-Briggs typology (which, for example, might classify someone as inherently an introvert or extrovert). Students can control their behavior, motivation and affect, and cognition in order to improve their academic learning and performance. Although students may believe that they can "only learn one way" or that they "are too hyper a person" to learn how to become self-regulating, there is an abundance of empirical research that shows that students can learn how to control their own learning and become self-regulated learners (see Schunk and Zimmerman, 1994; Zimmerman and Schunk, 1989). It is not always easy, but students should accept responsibility for their own learning and realize that they have the potential to control their own learning. At the same time, faculty can help students learn how to control their own learning by providing opportunities for student choice and control of academic tasks.

Self-Regulated Learning Is Appropriate to the College Context. In contrast to students in K-12 education, most college student have a great deal of control over their own time management and schoolwork schedules as well as over how they actually go about studying and learning. At the same time, many college students have difficulty managing this freedom in terms of the quantity of time they devote to learning as well as the quality of cognitive effort they put into learning. If students can learn to control their study time and learning, they will better adapt to the academic demands of the college classroom and will better balance those demands with the social demands of college life (Zimmerman, Greenberg, and Weinstein, 1994). In this manner, research on self-regulated learning may be more relevant to college students than to K-12 students. In addition, in contrast to traditional psychological research, which is often based in the laboratory and focused on nonacademic tasks, much of the research on college students and their self-regulation of learning has been done in ecologically valid classroom studies and has focused on actual tasks taken from real college courses (for example, studying for midterm exams in chemistry, biology, or calculus; writing an essay for an English class; or writing a paper for a psychology course). The ecological validity of the self-regulation research makes it much easier to apply to the classroom than some traditional psychological research. In Chapter Six, Stuart Karabenick and Jan Collins-Eaglin provide an excellent description of how faculty from a number of different disciplines have used ideas about self-regulated learning in their classrooms.

Self-Regulated Learning Is Teachable. Just as students can learn to become self-regulated learners, teachers can teach in ways that help students become self-regulating learners. There are any number of specific strategies for doing this. In Chapter Seven, Brian Coppola describes the many instructional strategies he uses in his chemistry classes at the University of Michigan. The most important idea to keep in mind is that strategies for self-regulated learning can be taught in any type of classroom context. They can be taught in separate courses or programs, like the one described by Trawick and Corno in this volume, or in general study and learning skills programs (see Weinstein, 1994), and they can also be taught in mathematics, science, social sciences, and humanities courses.

How Can Self-Regulated Learning for College Students Be Improved?

Each of the following chapters has specific suggestions for both students and faculty members about facilitating self-regulated learning. Here, I highlight five general principles for encouraging self-regulated learning, which apply to both students and faculty.

Students need to have greater awareness of their own behavior, motivation, and cognition. For students to become self-regulated learners, it is essential that they become aware of their behavior, motivation, and cognition by reflecting on these aspects of their learning. Self-reflection is not an easy task for most individuals. As Zimmerman and Paulsen point out in their chapter, students need feedback about their learning, in order to become aware of their strengths and weaknesses, before they can attempt to change their learning. Zimmerman and Paulsen make a number of suggestions for different "tools" students might use to get this feedback. Standardized assessment instruments such as the Motivated Strategies for Learning Questionnaire (Pintrich, Smith, Garcia, and McKeachie, 1993) or the Learning and Study Strategies Inventory (Weinstein, Schulte, and Palmer, 1987) also can provide students with feedback about their motivational beliefs and learning strategies. Karabenick and Collins-Eaglin describe how faculty in many disciplines have used these instruments and others to investigate their students' motivation and self-regulated learning as well as to provide feedback to students. Finally, many of the instructional strategies that Coppola discusses are explicitly designed to provide feedback to students about their cognition and learning.

Students need to have positive motivational beliefs. Self-regulated learning can be a very difficult and time-consuming process. It certainly takes more time and cognitive effort than simply reading and memorizing course material. Students are not likely to engage in self-regulated learning if they are focused on just completing their work to "get it done" or to get the highest grade. This type of performance orientation is not conducive to self-regulated learning, as Hagen and Weinstein point out. They show that it is much more facilitative for self-regulated learning when students have a mastery orientation and focus on learning and understanding the material. This does not mean that students should not care about their grades, it just means that grades should not be their sole schoolwork goal (see Pintrich and Garcia, 1991). Hagen and Weinstein and also Coppola suggest various strategies faculty might use in their courses to lessen the emphasis on grades and grading curves and increase students' mastery goal orientations.

Besides a mastery goal orientation, another positive motivational belief that facilitates self-regulated learning is positive self-efficacy for learning. As we saw in the case of Michael, learning was hampered by his low efficacy beliefs and high anxiety. Positive self-efficacy beliefs are not to be confused with general and global self-esteem or self-worth beliefs (for example, the thought that one is "a good person" relates to self-esteem not self-efficacy). Self-efficacy beliefs are very task- and domain-specific and include students' judgments of their capabilities to do a task ("I know I can do these chemistry problems"). Faculty rightfully insist it is not their role to improve students' global self-esteem and make them feel good about themselves in general. However, faculty can and should strive to make the students believe they can master the content knowledge and reasoning strategies that are used in their discipline. It is clear from an abundance of research on self-efficacy (see Bandura, 1986; Schunk, 1994) that students will have difficulty learning the course material if they do not have appropriate self-efficacy beliefs. The key word is "appropriate." Self-efficacy beliefs should be neither overly negative nor overly optimistic. Students should have fairly accurate, and positive, beliefs that they can learn and master course material. Both Garcia and Coppola provide suggestions for facilitating students' motivation and self-efficacy beliefs.

Faculty can be models of self-regulated learning. Zimmerman and Paulsen, Hagen and Weinstein, Trawick and Corno, and Coppola all stress the importance of faculty's modeling various learning and thinking strategies for students. One of the most difficult tasks for many of us who are faculty members is to make explicit the knowledge and ways of thinking that constitute our disciplines. Once we become experts in our fields, much of our disciplinary knowledge and thinking becomes automatized and is second nature for us. Students, as relative novices in a discipline, are not familiar with this knowledge and do not necessarily know how to think in the discipline. Yet we often lecture and discuss our fields as if the students were peers or colleagues and familiar with the knowledge and strategies of our disciplines. As Coppola points out about teaching chemistry, students can join this conversation at our level only with a great deal of help. By modeling our thoughts about disciplinary content knowledge, our own strategies for learning, and how we think and reason, we can help students become aware of what is required in our courses and help them become self-regulating learners.

Students need to practice self-regulatory learning strategies. Becoming a self-regulating learner is not a task to be accomplished overnight, in a week, or even during a whole semester. Students need time and opportunity to develop their self-regulatory strategies. Explicit courses, such as those discussed by Trawick and Corno, can help students get started, but students need to continue to practice and use the strategies over time after the formal course is completed. The opportunities and time can come from the student's own efforts to practice self-regulation as well as through tasks and situations that faculty organize in their classrooms. Moreover, in the classroom setting, faculty members can guide students through the tasks, deliver corrective feedback that helps a student see where he has gone wrong, and provide hints about how the student can get back on the proper path. Such guided instruction can be very helpful as students try to become self-regulated learners.

Classroom tasks can be and should be opportunities for student self-regulation. As pointed out earlier, models of self-regulated learning may be most relevant to college students and classrooms because there is inherently more freedom for college students than there is for most K-12 students. Nevertheless, the tasks that college students confront should be structured in ways that provide them with opportunities for self-regulation. As Zimmerman (1994) points out, students must have some choice and control over their learning if self-regulated learning is to occur. In this volume, Hagen and Weinstein note the importance of choice and control in fostering a mastery orientation in students. The provision of choice and control does not mean that faculty give up their decision-making power in terms of the course content or even in terms of the structure of exams, papers, labs, or course assignments. Instead, there are strategies that allow students some decision making and some control over their work while maintaining integrity of the curriculum content. Exam or paper assignments with a choice of essay questions or topics within a prescribed list allow students some control without resulting in randomly selected topics. Coppola offers other instructional strategies that allow students choice and control over their learning.

These five general principles do not exhaust all the things that students and faculty can do to improve self-regulated learning in the college classroom. However, they do provide an overarching view of the different instructional strategies and recommendations the reader will confront in the chapters in this volume. It seems clear from research on self-regulated learning, including the chapters in this volume, that the construct has important implications for college students and faculty. Models of self-regulated learning provide a very useful description of what good learners do in college courses. There is still much to be learned about what self-regulated learners do, about how students learn to become self-regulated learners, and about how faculty can help students develop into self-regulated learners, but the research presented here provides a good beginning. It is intended to spark more research and development about an important area of college teaching and learning.

References

Ames, C. "Classrooms: Goals, Structures, and Student Motivation." *Journal of Educational Psychology,* 1992, *84,* 261–271.

Bandura, A. *Social Foundations of Thought and Action: A Social Cognitive Theory.* Englewood Cliffs, N.J.: Prentice Hall, 1986.

Covington, M. V. *Making the Grade: A Self-Worth Perspective on Motivation and School Reform.* Cambridge, England: Cambridge University Press, 1992.

Garcia, T., and Pintrich, P. R. "Regulating Motivation and Cognition in the Classroom: The Role of Self-Schemas and Self-Regulatory Strategies." In D. H. Schunk and B. J. Zimmerman (eds.), *Self-Regulation of Learning and Performance: Issues and Educational Applications.* Hillsdale, N.J.: Erlbaum, 1994.

Pintrich, P. R., and De Groot, E. "Motivational and Self-Regulated Learning Components of Classroom Academic Performance." *Journal of Educational Psychology,* 1990, *82,* 33–40.

Pintrich, P. R., and Garcia, T. "Student Goal Orientation and Self-Regulation in the College Classroom." In M. L. Maehr and P. R. Pintrich (eds.), *Advances in Motivation and Achievement:* Vol. 7. *Goals and Self-Regulatory Processes.* Greenwich, Conn.: JAI Press, 1991.

Pintrich, P. R., Smith, D.A.F., Garcia, T., and McKeachie, W. J. "Reliability and Predictive Validity of the Motivated Strategies for Learning Questionnaire (MSLQ)." *Educational and Psychological Measurement,* 1993, *53,* 801–803.

Schunk, D. H. "Self-Regulation of Self-Efficacy and Attributions in Academic Settings." In D. H. Schunk and B. J. Zimmerman (eds.), *Self-Regulation of Learning and Performance: Issues and Educational Applications.* Hillsdale, N.J.: Erlbaum, 1994.

Schunk, D. H., and Zimmerman, B. J. *Self-Regulation of Learning and Performance: Issues and Educational Applications.* Hillsdale, N.J.: Erlbaum, 1994.

Weinstein, C. E. "Students at-Risk for Academic Failure: Learning to Learn Classes." In K. Pritchard and R. M. Sawyer (eds.), *Handbook of College Teaching: Theory and Applications.* Westport, Conn.: Greenwood Press, 1994.

Weinstein, C. E., Schulte, A., and Palmer, D. *LASSI: Learning and Study Strategies Inventory.* Clearwater, Fla.: H & H, 1987.

Zimmerman, B. J. "Dimensions of Academic Self-Regulation: A Conceptual Framework for Education." In D. H. Schunk and B. J. Zimmerman (eds.), *Self-Regulation of Learning and Performance: Issues and Educational Applications.* Hillsdale, N.J.: Erlbaum, 1994.

Zimmerman, B. J., Greenberg, D., and Weinstein, C. E. "Self-Regulating Academic Study Time: A Strategy Approach." In D. H. Schunk and B. J. Zimmerman (eds.), *Self-Regulation of Learning and Performance: Issues and Educational Applications.* Hillsdale, N.J.: Erlbaum, 1994.

Zimmerman, B. J., and Schunk, D. H. *Self-Regulated Learning and Academic Achievement: Theory, Research, and Practice.* New York: Springer-Verlag, 1989.

PAUL R. PINTRICH is associate professor in the Combined Program in Education and Psychology at the University of Michigan, Ann Arbor.

Self-monitoring is an important component of self-regulated learning. Students need to be able to engage in self-monitoring in order to regulate their own learning, and faculty can help students learn how to self-monitor.

Self-Monitoring During Collegiate Studying: An Invaluable Tool for Academic Self-Regulation

Barry J. Zimmerman, Andrew S. Paulsen

A primary goal of education from kindergarten through graduate school is to foster independent, self-motivated, self-regulated thinkers and learners. Today's information-rich environment can be a huge resource for students who are able to seek information from diverse sources, think critically about what they find, and select and integrate knowledge. The question is how students can become such proactive, resourceful learners.

Teachers know self-regulated academic learners when they see them—these students are interested in the subject matter; well-prepared; and ready with comments, questions, ideas, and insights; they are problem finders and problem solvers, unafraid to fail or to admit they do not understand, driven to rectify failure and to construct understanding. Identifying such students is relatively easy; the challenge is to develop a self-regulated approach to learning among those who do not already use that approach.

Instructors differ in their views of how such development occurs. Some assume that students' level of self-regulation is determined by their age and personality; others treat self-regulation as an idiosyncratic set of skills that each student must develop personally as he or she goes through school; still others assume that a common set of self-regulatory skills exists but are unsure of how to instill these skills. Recent research (for example, Zimmerman and Martinez-Pons, 1986, 1988; Pintrich and De Groot, 1990; Schunk and Zimmerman,

We would like to acknowledge the helpful comments of Junia Gabriel, Paul R. Pintrich, and Diana J. Zimmerman on an earlier draft of this chapter.

1994) has shown that a common set of self-regulatory skills does exist, that these skills are highly predictive of students' academic success, and that these skills can be taught.

This chapter focuses on self-monitoring, a fundamental subprocess of self-regulation. Academic self-monitoring refers to students' efforts to observe themselves as they evaluate information about specific personal processes or actions that affect their learning and achievement in school. From this information, students can assess their progress and make necessary changes to ensure goal attainment. Self-monitoring can serve as a tool for self-improvement by enabling students to direct their attention, to set and adjust their goals, and to guide their course of learning more effectively (Bandura, 1986; Corno, 1989).

A commitment to academic success at the college level places special demands on students because feedback from instructors is often limited to a few written assignments and tests during the semester. Under these circumstances, the consequences of failure are high. Students who are not self-monitors, that is, who cannot monitor their own academic learning and performance accurately on a daily basis, are at a great disadvantage. High school preparation for such independent learning is often very limited, and many students find it difficult to survive in college. This situation has led to implementation of learning-to-learn or mentoring courses at some universities (Weinstein, Stone, and Hanson, 1993). Instructors who teach self-regulated learning skills as part of their regular class assignments can also assist poorly prepared students.

This chapter provides an account of the self-monitoring process within collegiate contexts and describes how faculty can use self-monitoring to help students increase their level of academic self-regulation. We have organized this chapter on the basis of questions commonly asked about self-monitoring. Our answers are drawn from highly regarded theories and from research findings about academic self-monitoring. Thus, we provide both broad understanding and detailed knowledge of the self-monitoring process for college students and faculty.

What Is Self-Monitoring?

Self-monitoring has been defined lexically as, "the process of discriminating target behaviors and related events" (Kirschenbaum, 1984, p. 165), and as, "deliberate attention to some aspect of one's behavior" (Schunk, 1983, p. 89). Its primary purpose is to facilitate personal improvement and behavioral change. Self-monitoring requires one to attend selectively to specific actions or cognitive processes, to distinguish them from other actions or processes, and to discriminate their outcomes. Compared to informal self-monitoring, which involves casual observation or spontaneous reflection, formal self-monitoring involves systematic observations and judgments that reflect not only the present activity but also historical events (personal and contextual) leading up to and accompanying the activity. The specific information garnered through self-monitoring can then be utilized to evaluate personal progress, to discern patterns of causality, to initiate strategies or interventions aimed at modifying or redirecting the action, and to set realistic performance standards (Bandura, 1986).

In operational performance terms, self-monitoring usually involves keeping a physical record of one's academic performance (written logs, wrist-counter tallies, and audio- or videotape recordings for example). Such records can provide information about the quality and the outcomes of a student's academic performance. For reading assignments, for example, students can record in a daily journal such performance aspects as time spent, number of pages read, level of comprehension achieved, or resulting test grades.

Why Is Self-Monitoring Important?

Self-monitoring enhances learning in many fundamental ways. First, it focuses students' attention on a limited number of responses. When a student focuses on too many responses, no benefits are attained (Shapiro, 1984). Without a selective focus, a student usually cannot isolate the source of error, confusion, or inefficiency. So a selective focus facilitates an analysis of the student's role in any ongoing activity (Bandura, 1986). Second, self-monitoring helps students discriminate between effective and ineffective performance (Thoresen and Mahoney, 1974). For example, a student experiencing reading comprehension problems might discover from recording and graphing her reading sessions that she typically reads late at night and does not recall important details from the text very well at this hour. Third, self-monitoring often reveals the inadequacy of a learning strategy and prompts the student to find a more suitable one (Pressley and Ghatala, 1990). For example, the same student might elect to use a self-questioning strategy to improve her recall of important details.

Fourth, self-monitoring can also enhance management and use of study time (Zimmerman, Greenberg, and Weinstein, 1994). For example, time logs might reveal that the student did not budget sufficient time for reading course material in an earlier part of the day. Finally, self-monitoring fosters reflective thinking (Bandura, 1986). It can lead to better organization of one's knowledge, more accurate self-judgments, and more effective planning and goal setting for future efforts to learn (Lan, 1994; Zimmerman and Bandura, 1994). For example, monitoring reading behavior, especially during the beginning stages of a semester, can help a student plan and organize subsequent reading sessions, evaluate the effectiveness of new reading strategies, and decide on future course selections. Thus, self-recording can provide the impetus for changing a learning strategy and the basis for selecting and evaluating future courses of action. The type of personal change that can occur is often determined by which aspect of performance is selected for self-recording. This is called the reactivity effect (Shapiro, 1984). For example, recording one's reading time typically increases reading speed, whereas recording one's degree of comprehension can have the opposite effect because it prompts more rereading.

In addition to its impact on learning, self-monitoring can affect motivation.

If poorly motivated students are taught to self-monitor their performance properly, the resultant feedback can reveal unexpected progress, which in turn increases their perceptions of self-efficacy, outcome expectations, and goal setting and, ultimately, their overt motivation (Bandura, 1986; Zimmerman, 1989). For example, while monitoring their reading comprehension, pessimistic students might learn they are able to answer more summary questions than they anticipated. Such discoveries will raise their perceptions of efficacy for reading. Schunk (1983) found that students who self-monitored displayed greater self-efficacy, motivation, and achievement.

What Are the Main Psychological Components of Self-Monitoring?

There is considerable agreement about the overt features of self-monitoring, but theorists differ in their descriptions of various covert psychological dimensions. Information-processing theorists (for example, Miller, Galanter, and Pribrum, 1960; Carver and Scheier, 1981) view self-monitoring within a cybernetic system consisting of four stages: sensory environmental input (perception), comparison with a standard, corrective behavior, and behavioral outcome. Information about the effectiveness of an individual's current activity enters the system as a perception and is compared with a standard or goal. If the standard is met, no further actions are necessary. If a discrepancy between the input and standard is detected, the individual must act to reduce the discrepancy. From a cybernetic processing perspective, self-monitoring provides relevant information to the individual for making self-regulatory decisions.

In contrast to this emphasis on covert decision making, cognitive-behavioral theorists (Karoly and Kanfer, 1982; Shapiro and Kratochwill, 1988; Thoresen and Mahoney, 1974) emphasize the need for overt forms of self-monitoring, such as self-recording, as tools for adapting both covert cognitions and overt behavior to environmental conditions. They also emphasize the importance of self-monitoring environmental stimuli and outcomes. In response to the resulting feedback, two forms of overt adaptation are used: stimulus control and response control. Stimulus control involves efforts to avoid or manage problem situations (avoiding studying in a noisy fraternity house for example), and response control involves rewarding oneself for daily achievements (taking coffee breaks after completing assigned readings for example). Much of the work by cognitive-behaviorists has been directed at individuals with severe learning problems, such as hyperactivity, anxiety, writing blocks, and academic procrastination.

Distinct from both information-processing and cognitive-behavioral theorists, metacognitivists (for example, Flavell, 1979; Schraw, 1994) conceive of self-monitoring in terms of meta-awareness and meta-control of knowledge and of cognitive experiences and strategies. Experiences of meta-awareness, such as a student's realization that he does not understand text material he is reading, are expected to increase that student's willingness to make strategic changes. His initial awareness of personal ineffectiveness should, in turn, increase his focus on self-monitoring of the task and behavior sources. Metacognitive researchers have examined self-monitoring of such primary cognitive processes as attention, memory, reading comprehension, and communication.

Finally, social-cognitive theorists (Bandura, 1991; Schunk, 1989; Zimmerman, 1990) stress the importance and interdependence of all three major forms of self-monitoring: cognitive, behavioral, and environmental. Cognitive as well as external sources of information should be monitored and used to self-regulate learning and performance. Social-cognitive researchers have adopted the overt self-recording methods of the cognitive-behaviorists along with the decisional feedback loop favored by information-processing theorists. However, they describe this loop in terms of the processes of self-observation, self-judgment, and self-reaction, which correspond to the sensor, comparator, and corrective behavior components of an information-processing feedback model. The self-judgment and self-reaction subprocesses correspond also to meta-awareness and meta-control processes identified by metacognitive theorists. Thus, a student engaged in a reading task can monitor where she reads (environmental), how fast she reads (behavioral), and how well she comprehends the material (cognitive). The three sources of information reciprocally influence one other. For example, self-observation of reading comprehension can influence the student's judgments and reactions concerning reading speed and location. Similarly, where the student chooses to read can influence both reading speed and comprehension.

When Should Students Self-Monitor?

College students informally monitor many of their daily activities to some degree (for example, work productivity, procrastination, social conversations, eating habits). Formal self-monitoring, which involves systematic planning and overt record keeping, is seldom necessary if the task is easy, unimportant, or routine. To formally self-monitor such activities would be an unnecessary burden and, in some cases, could even be counterproductive (Zimmerman, 1994). However, when the student encounters a novel or difficult task or when a routine task suddenly becomes problematic (for example, the student does not understand a passage in a book), formal self-monitoring can guide personal adjustment, as we noted in the case of the student experiencing reading comprehension difficulties.

Formal self-monitoring can be especially useful in comprehending new reading material or acquiring new skills, such as material or skills in courses outside the student's college major. In more familiar curricular areas, informal self-monitoring may suffice, but it must be accurate enough to ensure that formal self-monitoring will be activated at the appropriate time, such as upon encountering a difficult textbook. For example, an English student might realize from casual observation that he is having difficulty making sense of the works of an unfamiliar author. Finding that he is unable to solve the problem using such informal strategies as reading more slowly or trying to increase his concentration, the student decides to formally monitor his reading by keeping a record of important events, characters, and themes. Ultimately, then, formal self-monitoring should be strategically planned and implemented on the basis of contextual cues and informal self-monitoring.

On What Does Self-Monitoring Depend?

In terms of cognitive processes essential to self-monitoring, students must first be able to discern and interpret subtle changes in their functioning. For example, there is evidence (Ellis, 1994) that speakers of a nonstandard variety of English who cannot discriminate reliably among their own word pronunciations will not profit optimally from self-monitoring in a speech laboratory. Second, students must be motivated by perceived academic benefits in order to invest the additional effort to self-monitor (Pressley and Ghatala, 1990). Such motivation has many cognitive sources, such as a person's goals, outcome expectations, and self-efficacy perceptions. If students do not believe that self-monitoring will be effective or that they are competent to do it, they will not self-monitor. Third, students must know metacognitively when and how to use formal monitoring (Paris and Byrnes, 1989). They must be aware when their informal monitoring is not sufficient.

The effectiveness of students' self-monitoring also depends on cognitive reactions to observed environmental outcomes (Kirschenbaum, 1984). If positive outcomes are revealed, students' sense of efficacy will increase and will sustain further self-monitoring (Bandura, in press; Zimmerman, in press). However, if negative outcomes are observed, students' sense of self-efficacy will diminish, undermining continued self-monitoring. There are ways, however, to increase positive cognitive interpretations of outcomes. First, asking learners to record positive forms of outcomes instead of negative ones can pay dividends (Nelson, Hay, and Carstens, 1977). For example, it is more effective for students to keep a record of successfully resisted distractions during studying than to record lapses in concentration. Second, cognitively accentuating the positive implications of adverse outcomes can also be beneficial. For example, attributing students' errors to an incorrect strategy choice will sustain self-efficacy better than attributing the errors to low ability (Zimmerman and Martinez-Pons, 1992). Thus, although observed task outcomes affect students' willingness to continue self-monitoring, the impact of these outcomes depends on intervening cognitive attributions and perceptions of self-efficacy.

What Are Some Problems in Self-Monitoring?

Problems can arise, first, when college students avoid formal self-monitoring because of inaccurate self-efficacy beliefs, for example, neglecting self-testing due to overestimations of preparedness for an exam; second, when students use the wrong standards to judge self-monitored outcomes, for example, relying on a friend's opinion rather than the instructor's guidelines as the standard for judging the quality of an essay; and third, when students react to outcomes in a negative rather than a positive fashion, for example, becoming despondent over an instructor's critical comments on an early draft of an essay rather than using the comments constructively to edit and improve the essay.

Self-efficacy beliefs that are too optimistic can undermine students' perceptions of the need for formal self-monitoring and can foster a casual approach to studying (Ghatala, Levin, Foorsman, and Pressley, 1989). Self-efficacy beliefs that are pessimistic can lead to half-hearted, poorly monitored attempts at learning or to task avoidance. If instructors establish a structured monitoring system for formally assessing knowledge and studying practices (as described later in this chapter), inaccurate self-efficacy beliefs can be exposed at a point in the learning process when students can correct them without suffering the irreversible consequences of failing grades or falling too far behind to catch up. Such systems can be designed to address individual learning problems and styles and to encourage students to self-adjust or regulate their own learning efforts (Zimmerman, 1989).

Problems also arise when students use ineffective standards for making self-judgments. Information about one's performance is constructive only to the extent that it is monitored with respect to an appropriate standard. The path to hopelessness and failure is marked often by unrealistic expectations for progress. In collegiate settings, academic standards typically are determined by the instructor. Research has shown that clear, specific standards for grading can serve as effective outcome goals of learning (Schunk, 1990). To achieve them, however, most students must set proximal personal standards to motivate their learning, manage their time, and guide their progress. Temporal proximal standards are advantageous because they provide an immediate basis for self-monitoring, a finding that brings to mind Lord Chesterfield's advice to his son in 1747: "I recommend to you to take care of the minutes for hours will take care of themselves" (Shannon, 1994, p. C8).

Students' inappropriate reactions to self-judgments can also cause problems. According to information-processing theories, the purpose of a feedback loop is to reduce discrepancies between an ongoing activity and a standard (either self- or situationally imposed) for that activity. Continued striving depends on negative feedback, that is, failure to reach the intended goal. Once the standard is met, many students may react by discontinuing their efforts to learn. This form of self-control has been termed negative because of its dependence on a negative view of feedback. However, when feedback is used to set new goals or choose new strategies, its self-control function becomes positive. That is, the feedback from monitoring need not be self-limiting but can be self-expanding, if students interpret its implications properly. Recently, social-cognitive researchers (Zimmerman and Bandura, 1994) have demonstrated the positive control function of self-evaluative feedback on college students' goal setting in a writing course.

Thus, certain problems associated with self-monitoring can be avoided if students self-observe at appropriate times, if they learn to set and readjust their standards effectively, and if they react to personal outcomes in a strategically positive way.

Do Students Need to Learn to Self-Monitor?

Effective academic self-monitoring is an acquired skill. When children enter elementary school, they do not make accurate self-evaluations of competence relative to classmates on academic tasks (Ghatala, 1986; Pressley and Ghatala, 1990), and their self-judgments of academic skill are inflated compared to their teachers' judgments (Nicholls, 1979). By the fifth grade, students can evaluate their relative academic competence with reasonable accuracy, and their self-judgments of academic competence correlate with their teachers' judgments (Nicholls, 1978; Stipek and Hoffman, 1989). There is evidence that structured testing experiences and teacher feedback during the elementary school years improve the accuracy of students' self-judgments of academic competence (Rosenholtz and Simpson, 1984). However, when formal testing criteria are not available, even older students are quite inaccurate when judging the quality of their own academic performance (Ghatala, Levin, Foorsman, and Pressley, 1989). Fortunately, students' self-evaluative capability can be enhanced through formal self-monitoring experiences (Lan, 1994).

Formal self-monitoring systems are planned and structured efforts to report the incidence of specific responses and keep easily interpreted records. Because novice learners lack detailed knowledge of the components of a mastery level of the skill they are learning, they must rely on personal uninformed estimates of progress, that is, vague feelings of knowing or doing better. In contrast, experts who know the key covert and overt components of the skill develop formal systems for self-monitoring. The selective focus and organized structure of formal self-monitoring instruments can be of particular benefit to novices because this focus and structure helps them to self-evaluate and self-regulate their learning through the eyes of an expert. For example, novices can be taught to define a vague awareness of "knowing" a reading assignment in more objective terms—perhaps "knowing" is being able to list the main points from memory after reading text passages. This list can then be checked against the text for accuracy and completeness, and the results can be recorded and compared with earlier efforts. In this way, subtle covert subprocesses can be self-regulated once they are redefined in terms of overt activities or behaviors. This kind of formal criterion of comprehension is more objective and helpful than informal personal impressions.

Formal self-monitoring systems also involve organizing learning tasks so that feedback is directly interpretable. For example, when textbook chapters vary greatly in page length, as they often do, reading tasks need to be segmented into nearly equal units before performance on one unit can be compared with that on other units. Chapters of varying length can be broken into page or paragraph units so that increases in reading speed across units will reflect growing skill and not merely shorter chapters. Many other collegiate assignments, such as writing or translating text from a foreign language, also have heterogeneous features, such as varying task length and difficulty, that must be "unitized" before useful feedback can be obtained. In this way, formal self-monitoring systems enable students with limited experience to self-observe, self-judge, and self-react to their learning in more expert fashion.

How Can Self-Monitoring Be Enhanced?

College students interested in incorporating self-monitoring into their studying should use a systematic approach (Kirschenbaum, 1984; Watson and Tharp, 1993). First, they must decide whether self-monitoring is necessary: Do they need to change or improve some aspect of their approach to academic learning, such as study skills, reading comprehension, or test anxiety? Second, they must determine what to monitor, which involves specifying a problem area and the behaviors associated with that problem. Third, students must decide on a means for monitoring the behavior, such as a wrist-counter or a log for recording. Finally, they must decide how to evaluate and react to the information gathered through self-monitoring.

As an illustration of the process, consider the example of a first-year student in an introductory history course with a voluminous reading list and weekly discussion groups. He may trace his difficulty in comprehending text chapters to an inability to answer questions in the discussion session or to describe a chapter in his own words. Having recognized there is a problem (step 1), he decides to monitor his reading behavior (step 2). He plans to keep a record of when and where he reads a chapter, how long he takes to read it, and how confident he feels about understanding the material after reading it (step 3). This initial monitoring exercise will provide him with baseline information regarding the nature and effectiveness of his reading (Shapiro and Kratochwill, 1988). He will then evaluate his current reading behavior in light of the monitoring information and decide on steps to take to improve his comprehension (step 4). For example, he may decide to use a highlighting pen to identify key points. Once an improvement strategy is initiated, he will self-monitor its implementation and effectiveness. If comprehension improves, he is likely to continue to use the strategy.

A recent study shows how a structured learning task can enhance college students' self-monitoring and achievement in a statistics course. Lan, Bradley, and Parr (1994) designed a monitoring protocol containing a list of the main statistical concepts covered in the text and lectures and a list of studying activities (lecture, text assignments, discussion, and tutoring) for mastering the material. For each method of studying, students in the self-monitoring group recorded the number of times they engaged in it, the amount of time they spent on it, and their perceived efficacy of using it for each statistical concept. The researchers found that students in the self-monitoring group performed significantly better on four course exams than a control group and than a third group that monitored the instructor's presentation of the material.

The salient feature of the self-monitoring condition was the presence of specific definitions of the concepts to be learned. By recording their method of studying each concept, students received continuing feedback about their own study activities, the time devoted to each, and their perceived efficacy in solving problems related to the concept. From this feedback, students could decide whether to review a concept, seek additional help, or classify the concept as having been mastered. The following student comments indicate the value of the self-monitoring protocol to the students: "Good tool to evaluate myself in understanding materials; also helps identify areas that I need to clarify"; "The protocols helped me realize what I didn't understand and how I could study to learn it more effectively" (Lan, Bradley, and Parr, 1994). Clearly, these college students perceived the academic importance of structured self-monitoring in providing interpretable feedback.

Teaching the Four Phases of Self-Monitoring

Self-monitoring skills can be taught in four phases: (1) *baseline self-monitoring*: students collect initial data about the academic activity in question; (2) *structured self-monitoring*: students self-observe according to a structured monitoring protocol prepared for the course by the instructor; (3) *independent self-monitoring*: students adapt the course-related self-monitoring protocol to their own individual needs; (4) *self-regulated self-monitoring*: students develop monitoring protocols for other academic activities on their own.

Baseline Self-Monitoring. In a history class, for example, an instructor might initiate the first phase of self-monitoring by asking students to keep a journal of their regular reading activities. Each time they read material for the class, students record their start and finish times, the number of pages read, the location and environmental conditions (for example, noise level and distractions), a simple measure of their perceptions of efficacy for comprehension (ranking themselves, on a scale of 1 to 5, from "did not understand" to "understood completely"), and any additional comments. This recording should take no more than five minutes after each reading episode. The journal then becomes a baseline that students can use to set goals for improving their reading. Instructors should model correct use of this reading journal in class and should encourage students to look for patterns in their reading behavior that might facilitate or hamper comprehension.

Structured Self-Monitoring. The importance of operational definitions is addressed in the second phase, structured self-monitoring. The instructor helps students objectify their self-monitoring by providing better behavioral definitions. Abstruse statements, such as "I understand Chapter Six," might be recast in behavioral form, such as "Can I provide a brief summary?" "Can I list the five most important points?" "Can I write a critique of the chapter?" "Can I lead a discussion on the main theme of the chapter?" "Do my important points coincide with other students' and with the instructor's?" Answering behavioral questions such as these compels students to replace vague notions of knowing the material with more precise ones.

Thus, by teaching the specific form of self-monitoring, the instructor can better guide students' cognitive activities during studying. In a class on twentieth-century Argentine history, for example, the instructor might want students to focus on important themes in each reading assignment, to generate critical questions, and to be able to discuss course material in terms of a set of organizing questions. Figure 2.1 shows a possible structured protocol for a reading assignment covering the relationship between President Juan Perón and the Argentine labor unions and the role of the Argentine military in national politics.

For the instructor of this course, comprehension is defined in terms of students' ability to write a summary and generate relevant questions. The self-monitoring protocol clarifies comprehension activities, establishes implicit comprehension goals, and provides immediate feedback on the reading activity. Instructors should provide a clear rationale for the selection of the themes on such a protocol, so that students can take over the self-monitoring process in the next stage. (Of course, the protocol format can be revised depending on course demands and student needs.)

Independent Self-Monitoring. Students are not fully independent in their learning as long as their self-monitoring remains dependent on an instructor's directions. Thus, while it serves important academic goals, the structured protocol is, more importantly, a means to achieving independent self-monitoring, the third phase of self-regulatory development (Zimmerman and Bonner, in press). The history class instructor, for example, might find that after three weeks of utilizing different versions of the structured protocol, most students are ready to develop the protocol for the next textbook chapter on their own. Students should determine the most important themes, based on criteria previously modeled by the instructor, and then they should prepare and complete a protocol based on these themes. Self-monitoring becomes fully independent when students can develop and use the reading protocol on their own.

Self-Regulated Self-Monitoring. To facilitate the self-regulated use of self-monitoring skills, the history instructor might ask students to develop personal protocols for self-monitoring of other learning activities, such as test preparation or essay writing. The hallmark of this fourth phase of self-monitoring is students' capability to generalize and transfer the general principles of performance structuring to new areas of academic expertise.

Conclusion

Self-monitoring is an indispensable aid because it not only uncovers areas of weakness in learning, it compels the learner to focus on whether or not his or her current learning methods are beneficial. Although self-monitoring will help learners regardless of their ability level, the instructor must take into consideration students' knowledge of the material and strategies, their existing goals and goal-setting skills, and their perceptions of self-efficacy for learning course materials. The self-monitoring system must be structured to increase accuracy,

Figure 2.1. A Structured Protocol for a
Twentieth-Century Argentine History Course

Week of _____   Reading Assignment _____

Reading schedule:

Date/Time	Location	Pages	Comment

Important Themes:

1. Perón and labor unions in Argentina:
    a. Located in text   _____
    b. Read   _____
    c. Highlighted   _____
    d. Took notes   _____
    e. Discussed with classmate _____

Comprehension Level:

1	2	3	4	5
Did not understand				Understood completely

Brief Summary:

Critical Questions:

2. Military involvement in Argentine politics:
    a. Located in text   _____
    b. Read   _____
    c. Highlighted   _____
    d. Took notes   _____
    e. Discussed with classmate _____

Comprehension Level:

1	2	3	4	5
Did not understand				Understood completely

Brief Summary:

Critical Questions:

to foster interpretations of results that indicate personal growth, and to replace inadequate learning strategies with better ones. When this occurs, students' perceptions of their self-efficacy will grow, and their motivation for continued learning will be sustained.

One note of caution should be sounded here, however. Self-monitoring must be integrated within a larger framework of self-regulatory skill. Unless self-monitoring leads to more effective goal setting, to greater awareness of the power of using learning strategies, or to better planning and use of an individual's time, its effects will be short lived. It is when self-monitoring plays an integral role in the use of other self-regulatory skills that students will experience a significant sense of empowerment and will reap the benefits of superior academic achievement.

References

Bandura, A. *Social Foundations of Thought and Action: A Social Cognitive Theory.* Englewood Cliffs, N.J.: Prentice Hall, 1986.

Bandura, A. "Self-Regulation of Motivation Through Anticipatory and Self-Regulatory Mechanisms." In R. A. Dienstbier (ed.), *Perspectives on Motivation: Nebraska Symposium on Motivation.* Vol. 38. Lincoln: University of Nebraska Press, 1991.

Bandura, A. *Self-Efficacy: The Exercise of Control.* New York: Freeman, in press.

Carver, C. S., and Scheier, M. F. *Attention and Self-Regulation: A Control-Theory Approach to Human Behavior.* New York: Springer-Verlag, 1981.

Corno, L. "Self-Regulated Learning: A Volitional Analysis." In B. J. Zimmerman and D. H. Schunk (eds.), *Self-Regulated Learning and Academic Achievement: Theory, Research, and Practice.* New York: Springer-Verlag, 1989.

Ellis, D. "Effects of Self-Monitoring and Discrimination Training on Pronunciation Change by Nonstandard Speakers of English." Unpublished doctoral dissertation, Graduate School of City University of New York, 1994.

Flavell, J. H. "Metacognition and Cognitive Monitoring." *American Psychologist,* 1979, *34,* 906–911.

Ghatala, E. S. "Strategy-Monitoring Training Enables Young Learners to Select Effective Strategies." *Professional Psychologist,* 1986, *21,* 43–54.

Ghatala, E. S., Levin, J. R., Foorsman, B. R., and Pressley, M. "Improving Children's Regulation of Their Reading PREP Time." *Contemporary Educational Psychology,* 1989, *14,* 49–66.

Karoly, P., and Kanfer, F. H. "Self-Management and Behavior Change: From Theory to Practice." New York: Pergamon Press, 1982.

Kirschenbaum, D. S. "Self-Regulation and Sport Psychology: Nurturing an Emerging Symbiosis." *Journal of Sport Psychology,* 1984, *6,* 159–183.

Lan, W. Y. "Behavioral, Motivational, and Metacognitive Characteristics of Self-Monitoring Learners." Unpublished manuscript, Texas Tech University, Lubbock, 1994.

Lan, W. Y., Bradley, L., and Parr, G. "The Effects of a Self-Monitoring Process on College Students' Learning in an Introductory Statistics Course." *Journal of Experimental Education,* 1994, *62,* 26–40.

Miller, G. A., Galanter, E., and Pribrum, K. H. *Plans and the Structure of Behavior.* Troy, Mo.: Holt, Rinehart & Winston, 1960.

Nelson, R. O., Hay, W. M., and Carstens, C. B. "The Reactivity and Accuracy of Teachers' Self-Monitoring of Positive and Negative Classroom Verbalizations." *Behavior Research and Therapy,* 1977, *9,* 972–975.

Nicholls, J. "The Development of the Concepts of Effort and Ability, Perceptions of Academic Attainment, and the Understanding That Difficult Tasks Require More Ability." *Child Development,* 1978, *49,* 800–814.

Nicholls, J. "Development of Perception of Own Attainment and Causal Attributions for Success and Failure in Reading." *Journal of Educational Psychology,* 1979, 71, 94–99.

Paris, S. G., and Byrnes, J. P. "The Constructivist Approach to Self-Regulation and Learning in the Classroom." In B. J. Zimmerman and D. H. Schunk (eds.), *Self-Regulated Learning and Academic Achievement: Theory, Research, and Practice.* New York: Springer-Verlag, 1989.

Pintrich, P. R., and De Groot, E. "Motivational and Self-Regulated Learning Components of Classroom Academic Performance." *Journal of Educational Psychology,* 1990, 82, 33–40.

Pressley, M., and Ghatala, E. S. "Self-Regulated Learning: Monitoring Learning from the Text." *Educational Psychologist,* 1990, 25, 19–33.

Rosenholtz, S. J., and Simpson, C. "The Formation of Ability Conceptions: Developmental Trend or Social Construction?" *Review of Educational Research,* 1984, 54, 31–63.

Schraw, G. "The Effect of Metacognitive Knowledge on Local and Global Monitoring." *Contemporary Educational Psychology,* 1994, *19,* 143–154.

Schunk, D. H. "Progress Self-Monitoring: Effects on Children's Self-Efficacy and Achievement." *Journal of Experimental Education,* 1983, *51,* 89–93.

Schunk, D. H. "Social Cognitive Theory and Self-Regulated Learning." In B. J. Zimmerman and D. H. Schunk (eds.), *Self-Regulated Learning and Academic Achievement: Theory, Research, and Practice.* New York: Springer-Verlag, 1989.

Schunk, D. H. "Goal Setting and Self-Efficacy During Self-Regulated Learning." *Educational Psychologist,* 1990, 25, 71–86.

Schunk, D. H., and Zimmerman, B. J. *Self-Regulation of Learning and Performance: Issues and Educational Applications.* Hillsdale, N.J.: Erlbaum, 1994.

Shannon, L. R. "Since Time Is Precious, Programs Try to Save It." *New York Times,* May 31, 1994, p. C8.

Shapiro, E. S. "Self-Monitoring Procedures." In T. H. Ollendick and M. Hersen (eds.), *Child Behavior Assessment: Principles and Procedures.* New York: Pergamon Press, 1984.

Shapiro, E. S., and Kratochwill, T. R. (eds.). *Behavioral Assessment in Schools: Conceptual Foundations and Practical Applications.* New York: Guilford Press, 1988.

Stipek, D. J., and Hoffman, D. "Children's Achievement Related Expectancies as a Function of Academic Performance Histories and Sex." *Journal of Educational Psychology,* 1989, 72, 861–865.

Thoresen, C. E., and Mahoney, M. J. *Behavioral Self-Control.* Troy, Mo.: Holt, Rinehart & Winston, 1974.

Watson, D. L., and Tharp, R. S. *Self-Directed Behavior: Self-Modification for Personal Adjustment.* Pacific Grove, Calif.: Brooks/Cole, 1993.

Weinstein, C. E., Stone, G., and Hanson, G. H. "Long-Term Effects of a Strategic Learning Course for College Students." Unpublished manuscript, University of Texas, Austin, 1993.

Zimmerman, B. J. "A Social Cognitive View of Self-Regulated Academic Learning." *Journal of Educational Psychology,* 1989, *81,* 329–339.

Zimmerman, B. J. "Self-Regulated Learning and Academic Achievement: An Overview." *Educational Psychologist,* 1990, 25, 2–17.

Zimmerman, B. J. "Dimensions of Academic Self-Regulation: A Conceptual Framework for Education." In D. H. Schunk and B. J. Zimmerman (eds.), *Self-Regulation of Learning and Performance: Issues and Educational Applications.* Hillsdale, N.J.: Erlbaum, 1994.

Zimmerman, B. J. "Self-Efficacy and Educational Development." In A. Bandura (ed.), *Self-Efficacy of Youth in Changing Societies.* New York: Cambridge University Press, in press.

Zimmerman, B. J., and Bandura, A. "Impact of Self-Regulatory Influences on Writing Course Attainment." *American Educational Research Journal,* 1994, *31,* pp. 845–862.

Zimmerman, B. J., and Bonner, S. "A Social Cognitive View of Strategic Learning." In C. E. Weinstein and B. L. McCombs (eds.), *Strategic Learning: Skill, Will, and Self-Regulation.* Hillsdale, N.J.: Erlbaum, in press.

Zimmerman, B. J., Greenberg, D., and Weinstein, C. E. "Self-Regulating Academic Study Time: A Strategy Approach." In D. H. Schunk and B. J. Zimmerman (eds.), *Self-Regulation of Learning and Performance: Issues and Educational Applications.* Hillsdale, N.J.: Erlbaum, 1994.

Zimmerman, B. J., and Martinez-Pons, M. "Development of a Structured Interview for Assessing Student Use of Self-Regulated Strategies." *American Educational Research Journal,* 1986, 23, 614–628.

Zimmerman, B. J., and Martinez-Pons, M. "Construct Validation of a Strategy Model of Student Self-Regulated Learning." *Journal of Educational Psychology,* 1988, 80, 284–290.

Zimmerman, B. J., and Martinez-Pons, M. "Perceptions of Self-Efficacy and Strategy Use in the Self-Regulation of Learning." In D. H. Schunk and J. Meece (eds.), *Student Perceptions in the Classroom.* Hillsdale, N.J.: Erlbaum, 1992.

BARRY J. ZIMMERMAN is professor of educational psychology at the Graduate School and University Center of the City University of New York and head of the Human Learning and Instruction subprogram.

ANDREW S. PAULSEN is a doctoral student in educational psychology at the Graduate School and University Center of the City University of New York.

Self-regulated learning involves affective concerns as well as cognitive outcomes. The motivational strategies of defensive pessimism and self-handicapping, in particular, can determine how students learn and study.

The Role of Motivational Strategies in Self-Regulated Learning

Teresa Garcia

Self-regulated learning is generally viewed as a fusion of *skill* and *will*. Skill refers to students' use of different cognitive, metacognitive, and resource-management strategies, and will refers to students' motivational orientation in terms of goals, value, and expectancies. Accordingly, the term *self-regulated learning* can best be used to describe the interface between motivation and cognition, following the body of research that has emphasized how both motivational and cognitive factors are important aspects of students' learning (McKeachie and others, 1990; Pintrich, 1989; Pintrich and De Groot, 1990; Schunk, 1989; Zimmerman, 1990).

In this chapter, I focus on two questions. The first is, What do self-regulated learners regulate? *Regulation* in self-regulated learning generally refers to students' regulating their cognition and effort by use of cognitive, metacognitive, and resource-management strategies. My purpose here is to highlight how students also regulate emotions, because students have not only cognitive, metacognitive, and resource-management strategies but also *motivational* strategies. The rationale behind the idea that students regulate affect as well as cognition acknowledges that achievement settings present performance risks and that performance outcomes have emotional consequences in terms of self-worth (see, for example, Covington, 1992; Garcia and Pintrich, 1994). Motivational strategies are a means for negotiating those risky situations that affect one's sense of self-worth. Like cognitive, metacognitive, and resource-management strategies, motivational strategies may be a function of one's expectancies, values, and goals for learning; however, motivational strategies are more closely related to the negotiation of the emotional outcomes of performance (regulating motivation), whereas cognitive, metacognitive, and resource-management strategies are more closely related to the encoding and processing of information to be learned (regulating cognition).

The second question is, How does regulation of affect influence the regulation of cognition, and ultimately, what effect does it have on level of achievement? In other words, how do college students cope with the stress and emotions that are sometimes generated when they do poorly in class, and how do some students seem to overcome occasional failures and become good learners? If students regulate affect as well as cognition, the regulation of affect may moderate the deployment of the cognitive, metacognitive, and resource-management strategies that we typically focus upon in our discussions of self-regulated learning. Here, I focus on defensive pessimism and self-handicapping as two methods of anticipating and negotiating the affective consequences of success and failure, and I discuss how these strategies impact self-regulated learning.

Strategy of Defensive Pessimism

Norem and Cantor (1986b) define *defensive pessimism* as "setting unrealistically low expectations . . . in an attempt to harness anxiety . . . in order to prepare . . . for potential failure and to motivate oneself to work hard in order to avoid that failure" (pp. 1208–1209). To illustrate, Khadijah is a student who has a history of above average performance; however, whenever an evaluative situation arises, she experiences a great deal of anxiety, and her head is filled with the possibility of failure. But rather than being paralyzed by these worries and low expectations, she uses the anxiety to fuel her efforts. Low expectations and anxiety motivate her to work harder. Thoughts such as, "Oh, I'm going to do poorly on this test," help her to marshal her resources and set her nose to the grindstone. Instead of looking back on her history of good performance and reassuring herself that she will do fine, she lets her defensive pessimism provide the impetus for cognitive engagement.

The strategy of defensive pessimism provides two ways for coping with the negative affect that comes with failure. First, if you set low expectations and fail, the pessimism (labeled defensive because it sets unrealistically low expectations) has allowed you to play through the situation in advance and steel yourself for that outcome. In this manner, it helps you gain some degree of control over the riskiness of the evaluative situation (Norem and Cantor, 1986a, 1986b). That is, if you tell yourself you are not going to do well in the first place, then you are emotionally prepared in the event that you actually do poorly. Defensive pessimism is a way of "preparing for the worst" and ensuring that you will not be caught off-guard when that risky evaluative situation turns out negatively.

Second, the increase in effort does make failure less likely, and the low expectations are often disproved by the actual success outcomes. Increased effort, therefore, also assists in negotiating the hazards of evaluation. In a sense, the anxiety we witness in defensive pessimism is beneficial, since it fuels extra efforts. Harnessing anxiety in this manner helps to bring about positive outcomes. The defensive pessimist is easily recognizable, she is the student with terrible worries about performance, who claims to be unprepared or dissatisfied with the quality of her work, and who yet ultimately and infuriatingly pulls A's.

With regard to self-regulated learning, defensive pessimists are likely to show levels of effort and learning strategy use that are on a par with those of individuals who do not use self-doubts to motivate achievement behaviors. High levels of self-regulated learning need not always be driven by perceptions of high self-efficacy and competence, as it is often depicted (see, for example, Kuhl, 1987; Schunk, 1989; Zimmerman, 1990); self-regulated learning may also arise from concerns about *lack* of efficacy and *lack* of competence.

Strategy of Self-Handicapping

Defensive pessimism increases effort to negotiate affective outcomes. In contrast, self-handicapping is the withdrawal or decrease in effort to negotiate affective outcomes—specifically, the positive affect stemming from high ability evaluations. Children learn relatively early in life about the link between ability and effort: how "smart kids" do not have to try as hard as other kids to do well in school (for example, Nicholls, 1989). This understanding makes effort a double-edged sword (Covington, 1984, 1992; Covington and Beery, 1976). High effort coupled with success is considered laudable, but high effort followed by failure carries devastating implications about one's ability. Self-handicappers are thought to be quite concerned about this effort-ability link (Berglas, 1985; Covington, 1992; Tice and Baumeister, 1990). The low effort shown by self-handicappers may produce poor achievement outcomes but may also produce a win-win situation in terms of affective outcomes, for failure following low effort may be attributed to that low effort, whereas success following low effort can only imply high ability.

Consider Paul, a star student in high school, who got high grades with relative ease. The results of his first set of exams at college shocked him. Instead of the A's he was used to getting, he was now earning C's and D's. He worked as hard as he had in high school but was now getting low grades. Imagine some of his thoughts: "What if I try harder but still get low grades? I got A's in high school and didn't work hard; now I'm getting C's. I must not be as smart as I thought I was." These fears help lay the foundation for engaging in self-handicapping. By strategically withdrawing effort, one can preserve one's sense of self-worth. Paul is concerned about the risk of working hard yet doing poorly (therefore implying low ability). By putting forth less effort, he can say, in the event of a poor performance, "I should have worked harder." Conversely, in the event of a good performance, he can proudly say, "I did well and didn't even study!" and appear very able. Other possible self-handicapping scenarios include taking on too many projects and spreading oneself too thin or waiting until the last moment to write a term paper or to study for an exam (see Covington, 1992, on such procrastination).

Note that self-handicapping is *anticipatory*. An evaluative situation is somewhere in the future, and the individual is working to construct circumstances that may serve as plausible alternative reasons for a possible failure outcome. Self-handicapping is a priori preparation for a possible failure, not post hoc reactive rationalizing for an actual failure outcome.

Self-handicapping has clear ramifications for self-regulated learning. If students differ in their degree of self-regulated learning, their low effort may not only be due to lack of knowledge about appropriate, effective strategies but may be driven by this self-protective motivational strategy. Self-handicapping may be related to poor achievement outcomes, but it is very adaptive in terms of affective outcomes. Assuming that individuals are hedonistically inclined to maximize positive affect, self-handicapping may be a strategy in which they engage when negative affective outcomes are imminent. The individual engages in activities designed to make failure attributable to events or circumstances and not to (or at least less to) his or her own ability and efforts.

Defensive pessimism and self-handicapping have strong implications for our understanding of self-regulated learning. The self-regulated learner is often portrayed as a task-focused low-anxiety student who is actively and cognitively engaged in learning (for example, Schunk, 1989; Zimmerman, 1990). Defensive pessimism gives a new twist to that picture. Defensive pessimists are highly concerned with performance goals and are quite anxious students, but they seem to be greatly involved in their learning since they use that anxiety to motivate efforts. Because of their characteristic high efforts, defensive pessimists may also show greater levels of cognitive engagement. These students are self-regulating their learning, but they use anxiety and performance concerns to drive effort. By the same token, the low effort and the low cognitive engagement by self-handicappers may also be seen as a form of self-regulated learning. Students may use the self-handicapping strategy to regulate their behaviors in academic situations, with the regulation being the *withdrawal* of effort in the interest of maintaining self-worth (Covington, 1984).

To recapitulate: students have motivational strategies that are related to the affective outcomes of evaluative situations. Motivational strategies like self-handicapping and defensive pessimism may, like cognitive, metacognitive, and resource-management strategies, be related to students' goals and values for learning. The high effort displayed by the defensive pessimist and the low effort displayed by the self-handicapper are thought to stem from performance concerns. Accordingly, these two motivational strategies may be closely related to an ability-focused goal orientation. Because defensive pessimism and self-handicapping influence the effort put forth in a learning task, these motivational strategies may then be related to students' use of cognitive, metacognitive, and resource-management strategies. Previous work has described the increase in effort by defensive pessimists and the decrease in effort by self-handicappers (for example, Baumeister and Scher, 1988; Norem and Cantor, 1986a, 1986b), but the quality and specific type of effort have not been addressed. Examining differences between defensive pessimists and self-handicappers in motivational outlook may provide insights as to why one group increases effort while the other decreases effort; examining differences in use of cognitive, metacognitive, and resource-management strategies may allow us to unpack the exact manner in which effort is being invested or withdrawn.

Research with Defensive Pessimists and Self-Handicappers

How do these two motivational strategies relate to such factors as intrinsic and extrinsic goals, self-efficacy, and anxiety? Defensive pessimists may be expected to report high levels of mastery concerns, on a par with "average" students, whereas self-handicappers should report relatively lower levels of intrinsic concerns. However, because of a preoccupation with performance, both defensive pessimists and self-handicappers may be expected to endorse greater levels of extrinsic goals. Defensive pessimists should report lower levels of self-efficacy and greater levels of anxiety relative to self-handicappers and to students who do not engage in high levels of either of these motivational strategies.

It is not so clear what relationships should be expected between cognitive and metacognitive strategies on the one hand and defensive pessimism and self-handicapping on the other. Defensive pessimists might report greater cognitive engagement concurrent with the high effort, or their worries and anxiety may stem from their reliance on less effective, "surface" strategies such as rehearsal. Withdrawal of effort by self-handicappers should translate to relatively lower levels of cognitive engagement in terms of cognitive and metacognitive strategy use. With regard to resource-management strategies, defensive pessimists should report the highest levels of time, study environment, and effort management, while the reverse should hold true for self-handicappers.

These predicted relationships were generally supported in a correlational study of 127 college sophomores. Students responded to a questionnaire about their uses of the two motivational strategies of defensive pessimism and self-handicapping. Defensive pessimists and self-handicappers were defined as students in the top quartile on the two scales, respectively. Comparison students were students who scored in the bottom quartile on both scales. In multivariate analyses that compared the three groups' levels of motivation and learning, I found that defensive pessimists did report higher levels of intrinsic goals, anxiety, rehearsal strategies, and time- and study-management strategies than did the self-handicapping students and the comparison students. Self-handicappers reported the lowest levels of intrinsic goals, rehearsal strategies, and time- and study-management strategies. I found no consistent differences in self-efficacy, extrinsic goals, and metacognitive strategy use among the three groups of students. With regard to performance, these multivariate analyses indicated that self-handicapping students had the lowest course grades and that the other two groups of students performed at similar levels (Garcia, 1993).

I interviewed some of these students, in order to describe how students with different motivational strategies prepared for an evaluative task (specifically, the strategies they used to study for a midterm exam), the expectations they had for performance, and how they reacted to actual performance. Basing my selection on responses at the beginning of the study, I chose twelve students: four self-handicappers, four defensive pessimists, and four comparison students, balanced by gender. The first part of the interview covered students' preparation for and affective reactions to the midterm. The second part involved presenting students with two passages from their textbook covering material that was tested in the midterm (one passage was about research methods and the other about sleep and dreams). The students were asked about their attention, understanding, and affective states during the "last time" they "went over this material before the test." The third portion of the interview was a stimulated recall of students' question-answering strategies and affect for the portions of the exam pertaining to the two textbook passages. The second and third portions of the interview address the question posed at the onset of this paper: How do students who differ in their use of motivational strategies differ in their use of cognitive strategies?

Preparing for the Test and Reacting to Performance. The twelve interviewees did not differ in the amount of time they gave to preparing for the midterm (the grand mean was 6.5 hours of studying spread over two days). Nor did they appear to differ in how they prepared for the midterm. When asked, "What did you do to study for the midterm?" most students reported going over the course readings and simply memorizing the concepts listed in their study guide. They may have used this method because the instructor constrained the task a great deal: students were provided with a study guide listing important concepts that would be tested; an optional "coursepack" was available, containing chapter summaries and key word definitions as well as copies of old exams; and the exam itself was multiple choice. Given the nature of the test and how much material was provided to the students, it does not seem surprising that the general study strategies for the exam did not vary. A typical response to this question was: "I went through the outline that [the instructor] had given us and wrote out all the definitions, answered all the questions, read through all the notes, and read through the outline in the optional book [coursepack]."

With regard to actual exam performance, students who were interviewed averaged between B and B+. Students using different motivational strategies but receiving similar grades did seem to diverge in how pleased they were with their grades and in their attributions for the grades. For example, a comparison student received a B on the midterm and rated his level of satisfaction with the grade at a 6 (on a 1 to 7 scale, with 1 being "completely unhappy" and 7 being "completely happy"). His attributions for his performance were: "From what I'd heard, the test was to be relatively easy, the class mean was a B-, we were given the exact information to study, and I was expecting an A or a B anyway. I know I can do better than I did, and I plan to do better."

In contrast, a self-handicapper who received a B+ and rated 5 as her level of satisfaction with the grade, ascribed these reasons for her performance: "If I had studied more, I think I could have done better. I was actually pleased, because I expected it to be worse." This response is in line with survey data indicating the tendency of self-handicappers to underestimate their actual course performance.

The high standards for performance reported by defensive pessimists are illustrated by a student who received a B+ and rated 3 as his level of satisfaction. When probed about his reactions to the grade, he explained:

> I had a lot of things on my mind going into the test. I had just gotten done with an econ exam the day before, and I was having trouble with my girlfriend going in [to the exam]. And when I was taking the test, there were like three to four where I wasn't sure. I had it down between two answers, and I found out that I had gotten them all wrong. I was really close to an A—I was like two points away. It was close. I'm not totally unhappy with it, but the lowest I wanted to get was a B+.

I also asked students to describe themselves the night before an exam and to describe themselves during an exam. Almost all the comparison and defensive pessimistic students reported studying (either reviewing calmly or cramming the material) and being anxious or concerned the night before an exam. Self-handicappers, however, seemed to vary in their concern over studying (two reported anxiety, two described themselves as calm), yet none reported any particular additional efforts the night before an exam. For example, one said, "I get very stressed and depressed and don't study. The night before is usually when I get the most stressed." And another commented, "Basically, it didn't feel that much different than your average studying night. I had a lot of other stuff to do the night before, also, so I was busy. Basically, I don't think I was in any different mood than I would be normally studying. I was calm. I hadn't anticipated the test being that hard, so I wasn't very worried about it."

Students generally were anxious during exams, although control group students and self-handicappers also mentioned being able to force themselves to relax. Self-handicappers did mention more frequently that when taking an exam, they tended to worry about and guess on difficult questions (perhaps due to their relatively lower levels of preparation). None of the defensive pessimists described themselves as calm. For example, here are three comments: "I'm usually calm on the outside, but the inside of my mind is racing, and I'm going, 'I don't know this!'" "I usually think I'm screwing it up pretty badly. Whenever I think I did well on an exam, I wind up doing worse than I thought I did, so if I say to myself that I really screwed it up, I actually wind up doing better, which is strange, but it's always been true." "Usually I'm all right, as long as stuff is familiar. There were a couple of things on this test I had no idea about, so that sort of throws me off a bit. I try to ignore those questions, and go on to the next question. Once I get done with the test and go back over it, then I realize I wasn't as sure about some things as I thought I was, and that's when doubt creeps in."

It is interesting that although the defensive pessimists were anxious and believed that they were doing worse than they actually did during the exam, they all expected to get at least an A- on the next midterm and to receive at least a B+ in the course overall. Thus, as the survey data indicated, defensive pessimists' long-term expectancies for performance were quite high, but their expectations during the evaluative situation were quite low.

Studying Textbook Passages. The second portion of the interview involved presenting students with two textbook passages that were covered in the midterm examination. Students were asked about their attention, understanding, learning strategies, and affect while studying the two passages. The first passage (P1) covered research methods and the second passage (P2) was about sleep and dreams.

Not surprisingly, most students reported that their attention wandered while they studied. However, only one of the self-handicappers (compared to all of the comparison students and all of the defensive pessimists) talked about being distracted by academic thoughts such as what the test would be like or how one could manage one's busy study schedule. While defensive pessimists and comparison students were concerned about learning all the material or were thinking about what the exam would focus upon, self-handicappers generally just daydreamed. Self-handicappers tended to be relatively less engaged in their learning, neither overly concerned with absorbing all of the material nor attempting to identify important concepts from the reading. Sample responses to questions about students' thoughts before the exam included the following:

COMPARISON STUDENT [P1]: Probably most of the time—not completely—because it was pretty late at night. I was thinking about how tired I was, how nervous I was about this exam, and I guess I kept thinking, "God, I have to do good; I have to remember all this information."

[P2.] Probably some of the time, because it was the last chapter on the test; it was the last chapter I was going through. I was thinking there was no way I was going to remember all of the information, especially the terminology.

SELF-HANDICAPPER [P1]: I'd have to say I drifted off here and there. I really have no idea. My mind would just wander as to what I did that day or the night before or last weekend.

[P2.] I guess some of the time to most of the time. Once again my mind would drift off in the same direction. Mainly whatever would correlate in my experiences in the past week; something that kind of correlated with what I was reading about; dreams I had, that type of stuff.

DEFENSIVE PESSIMIST [P1]: I'd say I was paying attention some of the time. I guess it also depends on what's being covered, if I think it's going to be something I'm really going to have to know. I was thinking about what I had to do for different classes, what I could be watching on television, what I could be doing with my friends at the moment. I'll think about anything. A lot of it is time management—what else I should be doing that night, which I probably won't get around to doing, in terms of other classes, studying, and stuff. [P2.] Some of the time. [What] I was trying to decide when I was reading this section, was how specific they were going to get on the test in terms of what they were going to cover. I was trying to relate it to past experience— like, how specific are they going to get? I concentrated more on the stages of sleep and what they were like instead of delta and theta waves. While I was skimming through, certain things I would repeat to myself over and over again, and then I would just phase out until I found something again that I thought I'd really need to know and concentrate on that.

With regard to understanding, none of the students had difficulties with the two passages. Students agreed that the textbook generally provided good examples and that the material in the reading selections was straightforward. Accordingly, all of the students generally felt comfortable with the material. Some reported being overwhelmed by the number of facts (especially in the second passage about sleep and dreams) and being pressed for time, but most felt that they were learning the information.

Learning strategies differed among students. Interestingly, self-handicappers tended to rely upon elaborative strategies and more frequently said they tried to remember the information by relating the material to their own lives or by relating the concepts to one another. This seems to contradict the finding of their apparently lower levels of cognitive engagement with regard to attention; it may simply be the case that when self-handicappers attend to the material, they do become cognitively engaged. All twelve of the interviewees remarked upon how much more interesting the sleep and dreams passage was, and interest may be a critical factor in cognitive engagement (see, for example, Renninger, 1992; Schiefele, 1991). Interest may therefore prove to be crucial, especially to self-handicappers' learning. Comparison students and defensive pessimists seemed to rely more on memorizing, defining concepts, and selecting/identifying important points, but again, this may be a function of the nature of the task. The instructor had provided review sheets and practice exams, and this may have triggered responses from the control and defensive pessimist students that were actually quite appropriate to what they expected the task demands to be. Representative responses to questions about how students studied included the following:

COMPARISON STUDENT [P1]: I just read it over, making sure I knew all of the terms, and [I went] over the terms in the section at the ends of the chapters. I'd say them back to myself.
[P2.] I went over the stuff in bold print in the book and memorized [it]. I tried to correlate the definitions so I'd know the differences between—I'd try to remember something in the definition so I'd remember what distinguished them.

SELF-HANDICAPPER [P1]: Just what we did in discussion is what cemented it in my mind. We divided up into groups and devised our own studies, and then used the terms from this particular section in relation to our studies. That's pretty much what made me remember it the most.

[P2.] I would try to relate it—trying to commit to memory—or try and find something that related to my personal life or something like that. Some particular example that I could think of that sticks out, that relates to it.

DEFENSIVE PESSIMIST [P1]: I tried to relate them to each other, and [tried] to put it down to one key word to define something, then I could relate it to the other word. I'll make up an acronym using the first letters of the words.

[P2.] As far as definitions would go, I would read the words in bold print, which had definitions along the side, and I would make sure I read over those. I would look at that, and skim the charts.

Answering During the Test. The third portion of the interview involved presenting the students with two sections of their midterm examination pertaining to the readings. They were asked to recount how they went about answering the questions and to recall their affective state as they worked through the exam.

While all the students reported using the process-of-elimination/making-an-educated-guess strategy in answering test questions, self-handicappers used this strategy more often than any other question-answering technique. Self-handicappers seemed to rely heavily on deductive techniques to identify the correct response, a strategy that may be due to their lower preparation. That is, if they were not as well prepared as other students, then they had to rely on making educated guesses, while comparison students and defensive pessimists, although they too used the process of elimination, also reported that they were able to identify the correct response immediately.

In general, comparison students and defensive pessimists had multiple answering strategies in their repertoires: process of elimination; thinking back on study materials; visualizing study materials; knowing the answer immediately; and when completely mystified, always guess the same letter. Self-handicappers tended to rely on making educated guesses and on trying to recall the material from the lecture or textbook.

COMPARISON STUDENT [P1]: Besides visualizing, I'll eliminate answers that I know are definitely not in there, and I'll have to decide between one or two, which answer seems the best to me.

[P2.] I just remembered, you know, how I studied, and then if I had trouble remembering a certain stage, I just went back and thought about, "Okay, well, last night how did I sleep?" and picked out the various stages, because I had more of a concrete example.

SELF-HANDICAPPER [P1]: I would go back to it. I would sit down, and I'd look at the answers, and usually just by looking at the answer, you can kind of remember. Because I would try and cement these things in reality; I'd kind of try and think back to the situation I'd put in my mind beforehand and that would usually bring it out. If not, I'd look at what sounded best, what might be good, and I'd put that down. Educated guess.

[P2.] I would try and go back to the part in the text, and if I could remember that, I'd go over some of the highlights—the main points. And if any of the answers popped up in that, I'd see if that was logical and I'd bring that back. Because the material was interesting, that's why I could do that—it would sort of stick in my mind.

DEFENSIVE PESSIMIST [P1]: Some of them just clicked because as I read the question, I remembered [the information] directly from the coursepack outline. The outline was definitely helpful; usually you don't get that in a class. If the outline wasn't available, I would have skimmed through the chapters again and compared the bold terms with the terms [the instructor] said we needed to know. He made it pretty easy.

[P2.] I tried to picture the lecture notes. And when in doubt, guess "C" of course! I'd use the Latin root, for example, with "parasomnia," thinking of the word "paranormal," and I concluded the right answer on that one. I mean I'm not going to remember everything from the textbook so I try to use what I've learned elsewhere to influence my choices.

In terms of affect while trying to answer the subset of test questions, both comparison students and self-handicappers reported being slightly nervous but not overly so. However, self-handicappers were more unsure about their answers and were concerned about doing well. Defensive pessimists showed the interesting pattern of simultaneously being nervous and concerned about not having studied enough and feeling fairly sure that the answers they were selecting were correct. Sample responses to questions about students' affect included the following:

COMPARISON STUDENT [P1]: Okay, pretty confident. I don't get really anxious. Once I'm taking the test, I just take it, so I wasn't thinking much of any-thing—just answering.

[P2.] I felt okay. There were a few questions that I left. I would think about it and try to remember, and I just couldn't. I eventually went back to them.

SELF-HANDICAPPER [P1]: A little bit . . . like I had no foundation under me.

[P2.] I felt okay. I wouldn't want to stake my life on the answers I was giving, but I felt fairly certain that I was doing okay.

DEFENSIVE PESSIMIST [P1]: I felt really confident about half of them, and the other ones I was like, "God, did I learn this?"

[P2.] I felt really confident—I knew what I was talking about.

Conclusion

In order fully to understand such phenomena of interest as dropping out of school or teacher attrition, researchers must study both "survivors" and "non-survivors" (compare Singer and Willett, 1991; Willett and Singer, 1991). By the same token, to fully understand self-regulated learning, we must examine both students who show high levels and those who show low levels of cognitive engagement (compare Garner, 1990). Adding motivational strategies to our models of self-regulated learning may be a way of gaining greater insight into the achievement of high-anxiety students, minority students, and of students labeled at-risk. These students' affective concerns may be taking precedence over the demands of a learning task. They appear to be engaging in motivational strategies that may increase effort and cognitive engagement, as defensive pessimism does, or decrease effort and cognitive engagement, as self-handicapping does.

As educators concerned with the motivational bases and the strategic aspects of learning, we must attend to the many demands students face if we are to fully understand the "whys" and "hows" of students' learning. The stark reality of the educational system as it stands is that being in school not only means trying to learn but also being evaluated. Strategies such as defensive pessimism and self-handicapping are means of anticipating and preparing for possible negative outcomes, and the results discussed in this chapter suggest that use of these motivational strategies is indeed related to motivation, cognition, expectancies for performance, and achievement. The research reviewed here suggests that students' regulation of their learning involves not only regulation of the encoding process and cognitive outcomes (by use of cognitive, metacognitive, and resource-management strategies) but also regulation of affective outcomes, that is, positive affect due to the maintenance of self-worth.

Defensive pessimism and self-handicapping are learning strategies in the broadest sense. As Weinstein and Mayer (1986) note, "the goal of any particular learning strategy may be to affect the learner's motivational or affective state, or the way in which the learner selects, acquires, organizes, or integrates new knowledge" (p. 315). Since self-handicapping and defensive pessimism have been shown to be related to both the learner's affective state and the encoding process, they truly can be considered learning strategies, and they can be important additions to our models of self-regulated learning.

The next logical step in studying motivational strategies is to examine contextual factors that evoke their use. Although defensive pessimism is beneficial in the sense that it helps fuel effort, and although Norem and Cantor (1986b) have shown that performance is actually impaired when defensive pessimism is interfered with, the anxiety that typifies defensive pessimism is certainly not something we want to encourage among our students. Rather, defensive pessimism seems to be a symptom of a competitive, meritocratic educational system: a symptom of which we should be aware and which we should try to redress. In the same vein, self-handicapping can be seen as a corollary of students' awareness that in our educational system, a student's value as a person is measured by his or her scholastic achievement (Covington, 1992; Covington and Beery, 1976; Nicholls, 1989). I suspect that certain features of college courses, especially high competition, grading on a curve, and unidimensional rather than multidimensional assessment (for example, a course grade based on four multiple-choice tests rather than a course grade based on two papers, a multiple-choice exam, and a group project) are more likely to engender high levels of defensive pessimism and self-handicapping. Of course, these are speculations, but they indicate the kinds of systematic research that are needed before researchers can confidently inform teachers about how best to promote students' positive motivational beliefs and cognitive engagement.

References

Baumeister, R. F., and Scher, S. J. "Self-Defeating Behavior Patterns Among Normal Individuals: Review and Analysis of Common Self-Destructive Tendencies." *Psychological Bulletin,* 1988, *104,* 3–22.

Berglas, S. "Self-Handicapping and Self-Handicappers: A Cognitive/Attributional Model of Interpersonal Self-Protective Behavior." In R. Hogan and W. H. Jones (eds.), *Perspectives in Personality: Theory, Measurement, and Interpersonal Dynamics.* Greenwich, Conn.: JAI Press, 1985.

Covington, M. V. "Self-Worth Theory and Achievement Motivation: Findings and Implications." *Elementary School Journal,* 1984, *85,* 5–20.

Covington, M. V. *Making the Grade: A Self-Worth Perspective on Motivation and School Reform.* Cambridge, England: Cambridge University Press, 1992.

Covington, M. V., and Beery, R. G. *Self-Worth and School Learning.* Troy, Mo.: Holt, Rinehart & Winston, 1976.

Garcia, T. "Skill and Will for Learning: Self-Schemas, Motivational Strategies, and Self-Regulated Learning." Unpublished doctoral dissertation, University of Michigan, 1993.

Garcia, T., and Pintrich, P. R. "Regulating Motivation and Cognition in the Classroom: The Role of Self-Schemas and Self-Regulatory Strategies." In D. H. Schunk and B. J. Zimmerman (eds.), *Self-Regulation of Learning and Performance: Issues and Educational Applications.* Hillsdale, N.J.: Erlbaum, 1994.

Garner, R. "When Children and Adults Do Not Use Learning Strategies: Toward a Theory of Settings." *Review of Educational Research,* 1990, *60,* 517–529.

Kuhl, J. "Feeling vs. Being Helpless: Metacognitive Mediators of Failure-Induced Performance Deficits." In F. E. Weinert and R. H. Kluwe (eds.), *Metacognition, Motivation, and Understanding.* Hillsdale, N.J.: Erlbaum, 1987.

McKeachie, W. J., Pintrich, P. R., Lin, Y.-G., Smith, D.A.F., and Sharma, R. *Teaching and Learning in the College Classroom: A Review of the Research Literature.* Ann Arbor: University of Michigan, National Center for Research to Improve Postsecondary Teaching and Learning, 1990.

Nicholls, J. G. *The Competitive Ethos and Democratic Education.* Cambridge, Mass.: Harvard University Press, 1989.

Norem, J. K., and Cantor, N. "Anticipatory and Post Hoc Cushioning Strategies: Optimism and Defensive Pessimism in 'Risky' Situations." *Cognitive Therapy and Research,* 1986a, *10,* 347–362.

Norem, J. K., and Cantor, N. "Defensive Pessimism: Harnessing Anxiety as Motivation." *Journal of Personality and Social Psychology,* 1986b, *51,* 1208–1217.

Pintrich, P. R. "The Dynamic Interplay of Student Motivation and Cognition in the College Classroom." In C. Ames and M. L. Maehr (eds.), *Advances in Motivation and Achievement: Motivation-Enhancing Environments.* Vol. 6. Greenwich, Conn.: JAI Press. 1989.

Pintrich, P. R., and De Groot, E. "Motivational and Self-Regulated Components of Classroom Academic Performance." *Journal of Educational Psychology,* 1990, *82,* 33–40.

Renninger, K. A. "Individual Interest and Development: Implications for Theory and Practice." In K. A. Renninger, S. Hidi, and A. Krapp (eds.), *The Role of Interest in Learning and Development.* Hillsdale, N.J.: Erlbaum, 1992.

Schiefele, U. "Interest, Learning, and Motivation." *Educational Psychologist,* 1991, *26,* 299–323.

Schunk, D. H. "Social-Cognitive Theory and Self-Regulated Learning." In B. J. Zimmerman and D. H. Schunk (eds.), *Self-Regulated Learning and Academic Achievement: Theory, Research, and Practice.* New York: Springer-Verlag, 1989.

Singer, J. D., and Willett, J. B. "Modeling the Days of Our Lives: Using Survival Analysis When Designing and Analyzing Longitudinal Studies of Duration and the Timing of Events." *Psychological Bulletin,* 1991, *110,* 268–290.

Tice, D. M., and Baumeister, R. F. "Self-Esteem, Self-Handicapping, and Self-Presentation: The Strategy of Inadequate Practice." *Journal of Personality,* 1990, *58,* 443–464.

Weinstein, C. E., and Mayer, R. "The Teaching of Learning Strategies." In M. C. Wittrock (ed.), *Handbook of Research on Teaching.* (3rd ed.) New York: Macmillan, 1986.

Willett, J. B., and Singer, J. D. "From Whether to When: New Methods for Studying Student Dropout and Teacher Attrition." *Review of Educational Research,* 1991, *61,* 407–450.

Zimmerman, B. J. "Self-Regulated Learning and Academic Achievement: An Overview." *Educational Psychologist,* 1990, *25,* 3–17.

TERESA GARCIA is assistant professor at the University of Texas, Austin. She holds a joint appointment in the learning, cognition, and instruction area and the quantitative methods area in the Department of Educational Psychology.

Mastery and performance goals can dramatically influence students' self-regulated learning. These goals are shaped in important ways by how college faculty organize and structure their classrooms for learning.

Achievement Goals, Self-Regulated Learning, and the Role of Classroom Context

Anastasia S. Hagen, Claire Ellen Weinstein

Many college instructors, when thinking about how to motivate their students, have asked themselves, "What can I do to increase my students' motivation so that they will *want* to learn the material?" and, "How can I get my students to care about more than just getting a good grade?" These questions address two different types of classroom goals that have been found to be related to achievement motivation: mastery goals and performance goals (Ames, 1992; Ames and Archer, 1988). When students have mastery goals, their primary focus is on learning, or mastering, the course material. Because they value the learning *process* itself, they often seek out challenging assignments and put forth more effort to learn the material. They also tend to use more effective learning strategies while studying. Students with performance goals, on the other hand, tend to focus on the *outcome* of their learning. They are primarily interested in getting a good grade in the course or, at least, avoiding getting a bad grade (Dweck, 1986). They also tend to use less effective strategies, since they are mostly concerned with the reward (getting a good grade) that comes after they have learned the material. For students with performance goals, learning the material is often seen as a means to an end rather than an end in itself.

Many college students have both mastery and performance goals. Indeed, it may be particularly helpful for college students to have both goals, because while it is important that students value learning the material, it is also important that they achieve particular levels of performance.

This chapter describes how mastery and performance goals are related to self-regulated learning, and it discusses how the classroom context might influence the goals with which students approach academic tasks. The chapter concludes with applications of these ideas in college teaching and learning. Much of the early work in this area of motivational research has been done with children rather than college students. Only recently have the theories been extended to college classrooms. For this reason, some early research done with children is briefly discussed to provide a theoretical and empirical foundation for describing the more recent research with college students.

Self-Regulated Learning and Achievement Goals

The following sections describe how mastery and performance goals are related to self-regulated learning and the role that self-efficacy (students' beliefs about their ability to successfully master an academic task) plays with respect to the type of goals students adopt. The relationship between mastery and performance goals is also discussed, with an emphasis on how these two types of goals together influence students' motivation and learning.

How Goals Link to Self-Regulated Learning. Dweck and Elliott (1983) compared the way students with mastery goals and those with performance goals approached learning situations. On the one hand, students with mastery goals are likely to ask themselves, "How can I do it?" and, "What will I learn?" Their analysis of a learning task involves thinking about how to best approach the task and devising strategies to help them master the material. Students with performance goals, on the other hand, are more likely to ask themselves, "Can I do it?" and, "Will I look smart?" The analysis of the learning task for these students usually involves first determining how difficult the task will be and then deciding whether they believe they will be successful. Because focus is on the outcome, less time is spent deciding the best way to approach the learning task. This often results in the use of strategies that may not be as effective as the strategies of students who devote more time to deciding how to best approach the task (Elliott and Dweck, 1988).

To illustrate the differences, consider a situation in which a college instructor gives an assignment to write a term paper. Students with mastery goals are more likely to choose a topic for the paper that is challenging to them, even if it is one about which they know very little. These students are likely to ask themselves, "What do I *want* to write about?" or, "What are some topics that I would like to know more about?" In contrast, students with performance goals are more likely to choose a topic about which they are already fairly knowledgeable. This makes writing the paper easier and increases the likelihood of earning a good grade on the paper. These students would be likely to ask themselves, "What would be the easiest topic to write about?" or "What are some topics that I already know a lot about?"

Another important difference between students with mastery goals and those with performance goals occurs when they have trouble learning complex material. Previous research with children indicates that when students with performance goals experience difficulty, they tend to reduce or abandon the planning and monitoring activities that might help them solve the problem. Conversely, when children with mastery goals experience difficulty, they tend to intensify their efforts and look for ways to overcome their difficulties (Diener and Dweck, 1978).

College students may show these same patterns of behavior, depending on the type of goals they have adopted in a particular course. For example, in a beginning calculus course, if a student with performance goals (and few, if any, mastery goals) begins to have trouble, instead of looking for different ways to solve the calculus problems, he or she may continue to use ineffective strategies or give up trying to solve the problems altogether. It is this student who is likely to say to the calculus instructor, "I just can't do these problems, no matter how hard I try." But when the instructor asks the student about the strategies he or she used to try to solve the calculus problems, it often becomes clear that the student gave up easily and did not try strategies that might have led to the correct answers. Dweck and Elliott (1983) suggested that students with performance goals who begin to have trouble may react with a premature, "I can't." When students reach this conclusion, they often fail to use metacognitive skills such as planning and monitoring, just when these skills would be the most helpful to them.

In contrast, a student with mastery goals who is also having trouble solving a set of calculus problems is more likely to say to himself or herself, "I'm not using the right strategy here. I know I can solve these problems. I just need to figure out what I am doing wrong." Because of their focus on mastering the material, such students often are successful because they actively look for strategies that will help them succeed.

How Goals Link to Self-Efficacy. Another important aspect of self-regulated learning is self-efficacy (Schunk, 1990). Self-efficacy refers to students' beliefs about whether they have the ability to successfully master an academic task. This is particularly important because the extent to which students believe they will be successful in a particular course plays an important role in the types of goals they set for themselves as well as in the amount of effort they invest in working toward these goals.

In achievement situations, students with high self-efficacy have been shown to actively participate in learning activities, show greater effort and persistence, and achieve higher levels of academic performance than students with low self-efficacy (Schunk, 1991). Even when experiencing difficulty, students with high self-efficacy tend to work longer and harder than students with low self-efficacy. Conversely, students with low self-efficacy frequently show less persistence and may attempt to avoid the learning situation altogether.

Note that the differences in behavior depending upon whether a student has low or high self-efficacy are similar to those for students with performance versus mastery goals. For students with performance goals, the academic tasks they choose to engage in are often based on how confident they are in their present ability (Dweck, 1986). If their confidence is high, they will seek challenging tasks and show high persistence at these tasks. But if confidence is low, they are likely to avoid challenging tasks and show low persistence in the face of difficulty (Elliott and Dweck, 1988). To put this another way, students with performance goals can perform effectively as long as they believe they have high ability. It is when they begin to doubt their ability that their having performance goals can be negative. Conversely, students with mastery goals have been shown to consistently select challenging tasks, regardless of whether their present ability is high or low. They are mastery oriented in their approach and show high persistence even in the face of difficulty.

It appears that self-efficacy plays a key role in the behavior of these two types of students. Students may adopt mastery goals because their self-efficacy for learning is higher. Students with mastery goals tend to believe that with enough effort they will be able to learn the material. Since past successes and failures are one of the most important sources of self-efficacy (Bandura, 1986), it follows that students who continue to work at difficult academic tasks until they master them will have higher self-efficacy than students who abandon their efforts at the first sign of difficulty and thus experience failure. The relationships among goals, self-efficacy, and students' behavioral patterns are summarized in Table 4.1.

Mastery and Performance Goals as Complementary. In earlier motivational research, it has generally been held that students have *either* a mastery or performance goal (Meece and Holt, 1993). Yet recent research on the relationship between mastery and performance goals has indicated that these two types of goals are independent of one another rather than opposite to one another. This independence means that it is possible (and perhaps likely) for students to have *both* mastery and performance goals at the same time (Pintrich and Garcia, 1991).

Meece and Holt (1993) reinterpreted results from an earlier study done with children (Meece, Blumenfeld, and Hoyle 1988). An interesting finding was that as long as the students had mastery goals, they reported higher use of self-regulatory strategies. Having performance goals was associated with the use of more superficial strategies (strategies designed to minimize the amount of effort required). The students with low mastery goals reported the lowest use of self-regulatory strategies and the highest use of superficial strategies.

These findings are consistent with earlier research indicating the importance of mastery goals in the classroom (Ames, 1992). Having mastery goals is generally associated with higher self-efficacy and higher use of self-regulated learning strategies (Garcia and Pintrich, 1991). As Meece and Holt (1993) suggested, having a "mastery focus may have its strongest impact in the absence of competing goals or motives" (p. 588). But an important question is whether college students are likely to be primarily mastery focused or are just as likely also to be concerned about earning high grades. In fact, it seems likely that a mastery focus is *required* in order to earn high grades in many college courses. As Wentzel (1991) noted, "performance goals are inextricably linked to learning goals in that it is impossible to obtain positive judgments of ability without first achieving some level of task mastery" (p. 190).

Table 4.1. Achievement Goals and Behavioral Patterns

Type of Goal	Perceived Ability (Self-Efficacy)	Behavioral Pattern
Performance	High	Mastery (seeks challenging tasks, uses effective strategies, has high persistence)
	Low	Helpless (avoids challenging tasks, uses less effective strategies, has lower persistence)
Mastery	High or low	Mastery (seeks challenging tasks, uses effective strategies, has high persistence)

Source: Adapted from Dweck, 1986, p. 1041.

With respect to college students, Hagen (1994) found a positive relationship between mastery and performance goals, which provides further support for viewing these two types of goals as complementary rather than contrasting. She also found that both mastery and performance goals were positively related to self-efficacy, but only mastery goals were related to the use of self-regulated learning strategies. This suggests that while students often have both types of goals, it is mastery goals rather than performance goals that contribute to self-regulated learning.

In another study with college students, Pintrich and Garcia (1991) also found that students often have both mastery and performance goals and that these goals together influence students' motivational beliefs, use of self-regulated learning strategies, and academic performance. Specifically, they found that mastery goals were linked to the use of learning strategies that require students to elaborate on what they are learning (elaboration strategy) or to organize the information in some meaningful way (organization strategy) (Weinstein and Mayer, 1986). Mastery goals were also related to students' use of self-regulatory strategies. At the same time, students with high performance goals also reported higher use of cognitive and self-regulated learning strategies as well as higher self-efficacy. Pintrich and Garcia concluded that while having mastery goals may be most beneficial for learning, having a commitment to earning high grades (performance goals) may also help students maintain their self-efficacy and help them focus on learning the material.

From these studies, it seems clear that college students frequently have a combination of mastery and performance goals and that both may be beneficial. While there are individual differences among college students with respect to their motivation, an important question for college instructors is whether student goal orientation is affected by the classroom environment or context.

In other words, does the classroom context encourage students to adopt mastery goals, performance goals, or a combination of both types of goals?

Role of Course and Classroom Context

As Ames and Archer (1988) noted, only a few studies have looked at how the classroom context might affect achievement motivation, and most of these studies have been done in the laboratory rather than in actual classrooms. The results from the laboratory studies suggest that it is possible to manipulate goal orientation through the instructions given to the subjects (Ames, 1984; Elliott and Dweck, 1988; Graham and Golan, 1991). For example, subjects in a performance goal condition might be given instructions that highlight their ability relative to others or that emphasize that the goal is to be the "winner," while subjects in a mastery goal condition might be told that they will learn a great deal or that the goal is to "do their best." The studies have shown significant cognitive and behavioral differences between subjects under each of these goal conditions. The purpose of this section is briefly to review these studies and to discuss their contribution to our understanding of the role of the classroom context on students' goal orientation.

Ames (1984) examined differences in children's behavior in competitive versus individualistic goal structures. An individualistic goal structure is one in which the emphasis is on improving and mastering the material. The competitive goal structure emphasizes competition among the children. Findings indicated that the children in the individualistic structure were more likely to believe that with more effort they would have been able to solve a set of puzzles successfully. These children also used more self-instructional statements, a strategy that can be seen as part of the monitoring activities of self-regulated learners. In contrast, the children in the competitive structure were more likely to believe that they had been unsuccessful in solving the puzzles because they did not have the ability to succeed. These children also appeared to engage in less self-monitoring of their problem-solving efforts.

In a similar study, Elliott and Dweck (1988) found that when mastery goals were highlighted, children were more likely to seek challenging tasks and approach those tasks in a mastery-oriented way, regardless of their perceived ability. A different pattern emerged when performance goals were highlighted, especially for children who had low perceived ability. These children showed a helpless behavioral pattern, characterized by avoiding challenging tasks, experiencing increased negative feelings, blaming mistakes on low ability, and generally giving up in the face of difficulty.

These studies by Ames (1984) and Elliott and Dweck (1988) helped clarify the psychological processes of subjects in two different types of goal conditions and provided important insight into how context might influence students' motivation. However, because these studies were conducted in the laboratory, it was not clear whether students in actual classrooms might behave similarly.

Ames and Archer (1988) examined the influences of mastery and performance goals in a classroom setting. The students were from an academically advanced junior high school and were randomly selected from one of their classrooms to participate in the study. Results indicated that students who believed that mastery goals were emphasized in that classroom reported using more effective learning strategies, tended to seek challenging tasks, and had more positive attitudes toward the class. Conversely, students who believed that performance goals were emphasized in the classroom had lower perceived ability and more negative attitudes toward the class. An interesting finding from this study was that an emphasis on performance goals in the classroom was important only if the students also felt that mastery goals were *not* emphasized. As Ames and Archer pointed out, "it was the degree to which the classroom climate emphasized mastery, rather than performance, that was predictive of how students chose to approach tasks and engage in learning" (pp. 264–265).

Wood and Bandura (1989) conducted one of the few studies that examined the effect of situation on the performance of college students. Building on the work of Dweck and Elliott (1983) and Elliott and Dweck (1988), Wood and Bandura examined how conceptions of ability (fixed versus acquirable) influenced organizational performance through influencing self-regulatory strategies. Students assigned to the ability-as-an-acquirable-skill condition were told that decision-making skills are developed through experience, while students assigned to the ability-as-a-fixed-skill condition were told that decision making skills are a reflection of an individual's basic intellectual abilities.

Students were told that they would be managing a simulated organization in which they would receive weekly orders for the production of furniture items. There were five different subfunctions associated with the manufacturing, each of which was to be assigned to one of five employees. Students were given the work characteristics of each employee, which included information such as the employee's preference for certain types of tasks. The goal was to achieve the best match between employee and subfunction in order to complete the tasks in the shortest time possible, thereby maximizing organizational performance.

Students assigned to the acquirable-skill condition maintained high managerial self-efficacy, set challenging goals for themselves, and used strategies designed to help them discover effective managerial decision rules. For students assigned to the fixed-ability condition, the longer they managed the difficult organizational task, the more they doubted their managerial self-efficacy. They set progressively lower goals and achieved less with the organization they were managing than the students in the acquirable-skill condition.

Wood and Bandura (1989) summarized their findings as follows: "We raised evaluative concerns about personal competence by the way in which complex decision making was socially construed. Other forms of social influence that focus attention on self-evaluation rather than on task mastery—such as valuational feedback, normative grading, competitive structures, and coercive incentive systems—can similarly have adverse effects on the level of interest, motivation, performance accomplishments, and creativity" (p. 413).

In another study with college students, Hagen (1994) compared students in two different types of college classrooms to determine how mastery and performance goals contributed to achievement. Each of the students participating in this study was enrolled in one of two different business courses. The primary difference between the two types of classrooms, that is, the context, was the degree of competition for grades. While competition is just one aspect of the classroom context, it often causes students to focus on how they are doing compared with other students in the class rather than on learning the material (Ames, 1984). Competition for grades is also a particularly salient aspect of the classroom context for many college students.

The low-competitive course was a business communication course in which students were given a variety of written assignments that ranged from writing a letter of inquiry to writing an analytical report. The course had twelve sections with approximately thirty students in each. In a part of the course outline entitled "Notes on Grading," the instructor stated, "Getting good grades requires a little practice—as does being good in anything! Don't be discouraged by a 'C' on the first couple of assignments. It is normal. The overall trend should be UP."

The high-competitive course was an accounting course. An instructor who had previously taught it commented that it is the course that "tells students whether they belong in accounting." The accounting course had three sections with approximately one hundred students in each section. The material is difficult and few students taking this course earn A's. In addition, 90 percent of the grade is based on students' performance on three exams plus a final exam. This is in contrast to the business communication course, in which only 15 to 35 percent of the grade is based on exam performance.

An interesting finding from this study was that mastery goals predicted achievement in the high-competitive classroom context, but performance goals did *not*. Conversely, performance goals predicted achievement in the low-competitive classroom context, but mastery goals did not. Taken together, these findings suggest an interaction between goals and classroom context that makes maintaining a mastery focus important in competitive classrooms. In less competitive situations, however, having performance goals is important. For example, in a highly competitive biology course designed for premed majors, it is the students with higher mastery goals who are more likely to earn the highest grades in the course. But in a self-paced medical terminology course in which students are allowed to retake exams, it is the students with higher performance goals who are likely to earn the highest grades. These findings suggest that successful college students may compensate for classroom context by adopting goals that are *opposite* to the type of context in which they find themselves. These goals may be mastery goals, performance goals, or both, depending upon the nature of the classroom context.

How to Emphasize Mastery Goals

While students often have both mastery and performance goals, it seems clear that emphasizing mastery goals in college classrooms is beneficial to students. Ames (1992), in her review of the literature on classroom goal structures, outlined a set of instructional strategies designed to support mastery goals. These suggestions addressed various aspects of the classroom context, including the types of tasks we give our students, the ways in which we share authority with students, and how we evaluate students.

Tasks. Ames (1992) suggested that instructors emphasize the meaningful aspects of the learning task (rather than more trivial aspects of the task), design learning tasks that are interesting and challenging to the students, encourage students to set short-term goals for the course, and support the use of meaningful learning strategies.

Authority. We can also promote a mastery focus in the classroom by helping our students develop as independent learners. This can be done by providing opportunities for students to make choices about course assignments. It is also important that we support students' development of self-monitoring skills by helping them solve problems on their own.

Evaluation. Emphasizing competition and social comparison among students can result in students' adopting performance goals rather than mastery goals. To promote mastery goals in the classroom, Ames (1992) suggested that instructors focus on each student's improvement and mastery of the material. It is also helpful to emphasize the importance of effort rather than ability and to provide feedback to students that the effort they put forth in the course is important. Along these same lines, it is important to encourage students to see the errors they make as simply part of the learning process rather than as evidence of low ability. Finally, it is important that we evaluate students privately rather than publicly.

Applications for College Teaching and Learning

The research and development literature in motivation and self-regulated learning has led to a number of applications for college teaching and learning. Each of these applications is designed to influence students' goals, motivation, and learning strategies by manipulating such aspects of the classroom context as instructional methods, learning tasks, and classroom climate.

Appropriate Goals. Students need to develop goals that are realistic ("I will read two chapters of chemistry tonight," versus, "I will read ten chapters of chemistry tonight"), challenging ("I will get to all of my French classes this semester," versus, "I will get to my French class today"), and measurable ("After studying Chapter Ten in my math text, I will be able to answer the review questions," versus, "After studying Chapter Ten in my math text, I will understand the material") (Locke and Latham, 1990).

Faculty can help students develop goals in a number of ways. We can model goal setting for class sessions or topics in our courses. We can discuss with students how to set goals for common class tasks, such as reading assignments ("What does it mean to successfully read the textbook?"), preparing for tests ("How do you know when you are ready to take a test?"), and completing homework assignments ("What is the difference between mechanically solving a problem and thinking it through?"). It is also helpful to talk about breaking long-term or complex goals into short-term goals. For example, writing a term paper can be broken down into a number of steps, and each step can be turned into a series of short-term goals.

Mastery Orientation. In addition to setting goals, students should also have a strong mastery orientation toward their learning. One way for us to facilitate this is to ask students to think about present or future goals and then to ask them to relate the course or topic material to these goals (Eccles, 1983). If students can generate interest in the course or in specific course topics by seeing how the material may relate to their present or future goals, it will help them generate a mastery orientation toward learning the material. Your encouraging students to think about how the course material relates to their individual goals has a more powerful influence on motivation than your telling them why you think they should be interested. Having students discuss their thoughts briefly in class can also help those students who are having difficulty generating interest in a topic or the course.

Another major influence on the orientation students will adopt is the way in which they are evaluated (Maehr and Midgley, 1991). Classes emphasizing competition and comparisons with others encourage students to adopt a performance orientation. If a student must perform better than others to succeed then it is reasonable for her to put her efforts into outperforming her classmates. Even though a student using this approach may achieve at very high levels, she often differs in her interest in the material and her feelings toward the course from a student focusing on mastery (she may feel the material is not as interesting as it would be otherwise, or she may feel anxious about the course). Classes emphasizing individual accomplishment, comparison to criterial standards, and cooperation seem to foster a more mastery orientation. This emphasis can be accomplished in a variety of ways. A very common method in college classrooms today is cooperative learning (Slavin, 1991). It takes many forms, but the common theme is students working together toward goals even if they will be evaluated individually. For example, two students can work together as study partners, going over homework, reading assignments, and class notes together. When they take the test, however, they are judged on their individual performance against a standard (criterion grading versus normative, or comparison, grading). Students working together could also work on different parts of a project but then be judged on their understanding of the whole.

Challenging Tasks. The nature of classroom learning tasks also influences student motivation to engage in meaningful learning. Tasks that are challenging and interesting to students are more likely to stimulate student engagement (Ames, 1992). For example, asking students to calculate the area of a rectangle is not as engaging as asking them to calculate the area of their dorm rooms. The instructional objective is the same, but the task used to accomplish it is more meaningful. It is also helpful to use tasks of varying difficulty, always starting with the easier tasks. This technique provides students with an opportunity to experience success. As a result, they are likely to have higher self-efficacy and be more likely to persist on more difficult tasks (Schunk, 1991).

Meaningful Learning Strategies. Many students do not know how to study and learn the material needed to meet mastery goals. This often results in lowered expectations, lowered motivation, and negative feelings toward the content and their own abilities. It is important for students to have adequate knowledge of strategies for general learning tasks and for learning specific content areas. There are many things faculty can do to help students develop and deepen their use of learning strategies. The two best instructional methods for teaching cognitive skills are modeling and guided practice with feedback (Bandura, 1986). There are many opportunities for you to model effective learning strategies while teaching your content areas. For example, when introducing the text or other course materials at the beginning of the semester, take a few moments to talk about how to read the text. Go over a few pages of the material and point out special aids provided by the author or publisher, such as underlining, shading, practice problems, examples, and so on. Model how to pick out the important information in the text (versus the supporting details and didactic material). While lecturing or discussing the content, identify methods students can use to help build meaning for the new information they are trying to learn. Describe methods such as comparing and contrasting, using analogies, and paraphrasing as you use them. Incorporate practice in using learning strategies into assignments and homework. Take a little time in class to discuss methods students are finding particularly helpful for learning the course material. These brief discussions can have a very beneficial impact on student learning.

The more students can take responsibility for their own learning, the more likely they are to attribute success to their own efforts. If students believe that their efforts will make a difference in what and how much they learn, then they are more likely to expend higher levels of effort in their studies (Elliott and Dweck, 1988; Weiner, 1986). If students do not believe that their efforts will make a difference, they are often less motivated to continue to try. Students need to know how to learn, and they need to receive feedback that their efforts are paying off. This has implications for the type of feedback we give to students. Our feedback should include observations about students' effort and, when appropriate, their improvement. For example, rather than limiting feedback given to individual students after their second exam to their performance on that exam, feedback at that time could also include information about progress the student has made since the first exam. Helping students understand that their efforts are making a difference contributes to more positive feelings and promotes a willingness to persist when a problem or failure does occur.

Conclusion

Mastery and performance goals, self-efficacy, and self-regulated learning are related to one another, and these relationships seem to be influenced by classroom context. Students can hold both mastery and performance goals, and one influence on which type is dominant is classroom context. College instructors can promote a mastery focus in their classrooms in many ways. For instance, instructors can emphasize effort over ability, encourage students to focus on their own individual improvement, show students how to set appropriate task goals, encourage students to relate learning the content to their goals for their futures, and model learning strategies for students. In these ways, instructors can begin to answer the typical educators' questions posed at the beginning of the chapter: "What can I do to increase my students' motivation so that they will *want* to learn the material?" and, "How can I get my students to care about more than just getting a good grade?"

References

Ames, C. "Achievement Attributions and Self-Instructions Under Competitive and Individualistic Goal Structures." *Journal of Educational Psychology,* 1984, *76,* 478–487.

Ames, C. "Classrooms: Goals, Structures, and Student Motivation." *Journal of Educational Psychology,* 1992, *84,* 261–271.

Ames, C., and Archer, J. "Achievement Goals in the Classroom: Students' Learning Strategies and Motivation Processes." *Journal of Educational Psychology,* 1988, *80,* 260–267.

Bandura, A. *Social Foundations of Thought and Action: A Social Cognitive Theory.* Englewood Cliffs, N.J.: Prentice Hall, 1986.

Diener, C. I., and Dweck, C. S. "An Analysis of Learned Helplessness: Continuous Changes in Performance, Strategy, and Achievement Cognitions Following Failure." *Journal of Personality and Social Psychology,* 1978, *36,* 451–462.

Dweck, C. S. "Motivational Processes Affecting Learning." *American Psychologist,* 1986, *41,* 1040–1048.

Dweck, C. S., and Elliott, E. S. "Achievement Motivation." In P. H. Mussen and E. M. Hetherington (eds.), *Handbook of Child Psychology.* Vol. 4. *Socialization, Personality, and Social Development.* New York: Wiley, 1983.

Eccles, J. "Expectancies, Values and Academic Behaviors." In J. T. Spence (ed.), *Achievement and Achievement Motives: Psychological and Sociological Approaches.* New York: Freeman, 1983.

Elliott, E. S., and Dweck, C. S. "Goals: An Approach to Motivation and Achievement." *Journal of Personality and Social Psychology,* 1988, *54,* 5–12.

Garcia, T., and Pintrich, P. R. *Student Motivation and Self-Regulated Learning: A LISREL Model.* Paper presented at the annual meeting of the American Educational Research Association, Chicago, Apr. 1991.

Graham, S., and Golan, S. "Motivational Influences on Cognition: Task Involvement, Ego Involvement, and Depth of Information Processing." *Journal of Educational Psychology,* 1991, *83,* 187–194.

Hagen, A. S. *Achievement Motivation Processes and the Role of Classroom Context.* Paper presented at the annual meeting of the American Educational Research Association, New Orleans, Apr. 1994.

Locke, E. A., and Latham, G. P. *A Theory of Goal Setting & Task Performance*. Englewood Cliffs, N.J.: Prentice Hall, 1990.

Maehr, M. L., and Midgley, C. "Enhancing Student Motivation: A Schoolwide Approach." *Educational Psychologist*, 1991, *26*, 399–427.

Meece, J. L., Blumenfeld, P. C., and Hoyle, R. H. "Students' Goal Orientations and Cognitive Engagement in Classroom Activities." *Journal of Educational Psychology*, 1988, *80*, 514–523.

Meece, J. L., and Holt, K. "A Pattern Analysis of Students' Achievement Goals." *Journal of Educational Psychology*, 1993, *85*, 582–590.

Pintrich, P. R., and Garcia, T. "Student Goal Orientation and Self-Regulation in the College Classroom." In M. L. Maehr and P. R. Pintrich (eds.), *Advances in Motivation and Achievement*. Vol. 7: *Goals and Self-Regulatory Processes*. Greenwich, Conn.: JAI Press, 1991.

Schunk, D. H. "Goal Setting and Self-Efficacy During Self-Regulated Learning." *Educational Psychologist*, 1990, *25*, 71–86.

Schunk, D. H. "Self-Efficacy and Academic Motivation." *Educational Psychologist*, 1991, *26*, 207–231.

Slavin, R. E. "Synthesis of Research on Cooperative Learning." *Educational Leadership*, Feb. 1991, *48*, 71–77.

Weiner, B. *An Attributional Theory of Achievement Motivation and Emotion*. New York: Springer-Verlag, 1986.

Weinstein, C. E., and Mayer, R. E. "The Teaching of Learning Strategies." In M. C. Wittrock (ed.), *Handbook of Research on Teaching*. (3rd ed.) New York: Macmillan, 1986.

Wentzel, K. R. "Social and Academic Goals at School: Motivation and Achievement in Context." In M. L. Maehr and P. R. Pintrich (eds.), *Advances in Motivation and Achievement*. Vol. 7: *Goals and Self-Regulatory Processes*. Greenwich, Conn.: JAI Press, 1991.

Wood, R., and Bandura, A. "Impact of Conceptions of Ability on Self-Regulatory Mechanisms and Complex Decision Making." *Journal of Personality and Social Psychology*, 1989, *56*, 407–415.

ANASTASIA S. HAGEN is visiting assistant professor in the Department of Educational Studies at the University of Delaware.

CLAIRE ELLEN WEINSTEIN is professor in the Department of Educational Psychology and director of the Cognitive Learning Strategies Project at the University of Texas, Austin.

Urban community college students have many needs. A program that teaches them how to regulate and control their behavior, cognition, and affect can be a particularly important resource for them.

Expanding the Volitional Resources of Urban Community College Students

LaVergne Trawick, Lyn Corno

Over the past three decades, community colleges have responded to calls to admit underserved segments of the U.S. population—including minorities, immigrants, women, adults, and individuals with high school equivalency certificates, among others. Thus, community colleges have come to serve as the entry point into higher education for students who have historically been excluded. The current diversity of the community college student population is indicated by 1990 data from the American Association of Community Colleges (1993):

Forty-two percent of African American, 52 percent of American Indian, 38 percent of Asian American, 55 percent of Hispanic, 37 percent of white, and 19 percent of nonresident alien students in higher education attended community colleges.
Thirty-seven percent of community college students are twenty-five years of age or older.
Fifty-eight percent of community college students are women.
Sixty-four percent of community college students attend college on a part-time basis.

Although this increased diversity is to be lauded, at the same time, a more diverse student body presents numerous academic challenges. One report

This research was partially supported by a Spencer Foundation Dissertation Year Fellowship awarded to LaVergne Trawick.

concerning the academic preparation of students in community colleges reveals that in the 1980s, the American College Testing program mean standard score for all college students was above 18 on a scale ranging from 1 to 36. The mean standard score was below 16 for community college enrollees (Alkin, 1992). As increasing numbers of U.S. community colleges have opened their doors to all students with high school credentials or the equivalent, many eager students have enrolled (Cross, 1976). Upon entry to postsecondary institutions, they often experience learning difficulty and may have trouble in coursework. One possible factor in this typically downward spiral of events may be students' limited exposure to effective strategies for managing learning-related effort (that is, self- and resource management). Community college students may therefore benefit from assistance in how to protect their intentions to learn in the face of difficult tasks and competing intentions or other distractions.

In a survey at one large urban community college (Trawick, 1990), many students reported that they had worked quite diligently to attain the status of high school graduate. To do so, many attended numerous remedial courses. Others were involved in life events that had made it difficult to attain this status and/or had been told that they probably would not graduate from high school. Additionally, students sometimes verbalized unclear notions of effort. For example, some reported that they often "intended" to study, but never "got around to it." A variation of this effort formula was verbalized as, "I'll have to try harder," but the exact actions involved in increased effort were often less specified. In response to the question, "What exactly will you do more of (or differently) to improve your grades?" students tended to describe a global idea of effort akin to a notion of willpower, and to communicate a belief that sheer persistence and "showing up" would lead to academic success.

From the perspectives of some faculty, students reportedly engaged in "ineffective" effort. They set unrealistic deadlines for completing make-up assignments or procrastinated and turned in assignments done hastily. Again, the concern was voiced by the faculty that community college students may be uncertain about the relationship between their behavior and their academic success.

In academic situations, effort management or volitional resources can be used to build learning skills gradually and to control or refocus the anxious responses that often accompany thwarted intellectual efforts (Zimmerman and Schunk, 1989; Corno, 1993). Rather than providing opportunities for effort-management skills to develop, however, traditional college coursework generally assumes the presence of such skills or predispositions. Community college students may receive little advice on how to study or to negotiate the particular demands of college. If volitional resources could be enhanced in students who choose to pursue a college education but have little precollegiate preparation, they might then be able to pass rather than fail their early courses and to derive the accomplishments they seek. How a community college might help students expand their volitional resources with respect to academic work is the major issue in this chapter.

Volition and Academic Self-Regulation

Recent research has addressed similarities between modern conceptions of volition and the processes of academic self-regulation (see, for example, Corno, 1993; Kuhl, 1985). Self-regulation is generally defined to include the goal-protecting and resource-management processes known as volitional control *along with* motivational factors such as goal setting, success expectations, and deep levels of cognitive involvement in learning (Schunk and Zimmerman, 1994; Zimmerman and Schunk, 1989). Work by Zimmerman and Martinez-Pons (1988) and Pintrich and colleagues (Pintrich, 1990; Pintrich and De Groot, 1990), in particular, has examined a range of cognitive, motivational, and volitional strategies reported by students in correlational studies. This research suggests that different aspects of expressed strategy play important roles in academic achievement. Efficacy or high expectations for success and other motivational factors aid students in goal setting and in increased goal-related effort. Volitional control and goal-related cognition help students to maintain such efforts in the face of difficulty and other sources of distraction.

Self-regulated learning research as promoted by Zimmerman (1989) embraces a social-cognitive perspective based on the work of Bandura (1977, 1986). This perspective differs from theories of volitional control in its emphasis on planning or decision-making processes rather than postdecisional implementation or follow-through (see Corno and Kanfer, 1993). Thus, although most existing work on self-regulated learning begins to put volition into relation with motivation, it has not done enough to address the growing understanding that motivation tells only part of the story in academic learning and performance.

Students differ in such motivational factors as self-confidence in their own abilities, and such factors exert demonstrable influence on both motivated behavior and performance (Schunk, 1991). But many students who appear confident of their capabilities and who do work hard in school still perform poorly. Our experience suggests that the *kinds* of efforts such students make tend to be ineffective or unsustained, and that their conceptions of *how* to put forth effort related to schoolwork belie an understanding of the most relevant variables. Thus, helping students become literate about schooling ought also to help them establish productive work patterns that may be sustained when necessary (Corno, 1989b).

The significant body of research that exists on cognitive strategies in educational psychology (for example, Pressley and Levin, 1983) can be related to strategy research based on theories of volition and social cognition. A recurring result in studies of strategy induction with students is the difficulty of obtaining transfer; students who learn strategies during training do not automatically apply them in subsequent schoolwork (Pressley, Borkowski, and Schneider, 1989). When transfer does occur, it seems to be fostered by attention to issues of self-regulation and control during training or instruction (Dole, Duffy, Roehler, and Pearson, 1991; Paris and Winograd, 1990). Thus, new iterations of strategy research may need to give more weight to volitional strategies as potential vehicles for facilitating the application of other strategies.

Six volitional strategies identified by Kuhl (1985) have been applied by Corno (1989a, 1993) to academic situations. Figure 5.1 presents Kuhl's taxonomy adapted for purposes of the present discussion, as well as a definition and an example of a hypothetical student response to illustrate each category. Covert volitional control involves using basic metacognitive strategies for selectively attending to, encoding, and processing relevant information, as well as using motivation and emotion control strategies to promote intended actions. Overt volitional control involves managing task situations along with social aspects of the academic environment. Such strategies are hypothesized to assist individuals in accomplishing academic tasks when they are confronted with personal and environmental distractions. These strategies have a long research history in studies of cognitive-behavior modification (for example, Meichenbaum, 1977), and their concrete nature makes them relatively easy to use. The covert strategies, in contrast, are abstract and require more complex, internal reflection. (The strategies in Figure 5.1 pertaining to encoding control and information-processing control were not taught during the volitional enhancement program described in this chapter, due to institutional constraints.)

Thus, modern social-constructivist theory (Bandura, 1986; Vygotsky, 1962) centrally acknowledges the contribution of social interaction to human thought and behavior as well as the influence of cognition (including thoughts, beliefs, and perceptions) on human motivation and behavior. Self-regulation is viewed as socially influenced and cognitively mediated. The acquisition of self-regulation strategies derives from a gradual process in which a student's knowledge about self-as-learner becomes internalized through a combination of experiences involving instructors' teaching and modeling and the student's own use of internal speech to guide behavior, of self-observation, of opportunities to receive feedback about his or her performance, and of practice. Intervention programs directed at one or more of three purposes—improving volitional or self-regulation strategies in clinical populations (Meichenbaum, 1972, 1977), instructing college students using participant-modeling procedures (Shapiro, 1988), and offering learning strategies instruction (Collins and others, 1981; Weinstein and Underwood, 1985)—have all reported positive outcomes based on the use of such experiences (see Weinstein and Mayer, 1986, for a review). The program described in this chapter involves all three purposes.

Volitional Enhancement Program

The volitional enhancement program we developed for use with community college students consisted of four seventy-minute group sessions led by an instructor, one session during each week of a four-week period. It provided instruction and practice in monitoring and controlling both external and internal aspects of students' learning environments. In this program, the external aspects

Figure 5.1. Categories, Definitions, and Examples of Volitional Strategies

I. Covert processes of self-control

    A. Cognition control: managing the cognitive aspects of a task

        1. Attention control

           Definition: statements indicating student efforts to give selective attention to task-relevant information

           Example: "I'll try to make myself concentrate more on the work than letting my mind wander off somewhere else."

        2. Encoding control

           Definition: statements indicating student efforts to act as if some parts of the task are more important to understand and act upon than others

           Example: "I'd go over the test and see where I made mistakes ... go over that same test that I just had. I go over my notes, make sure I know what's going to be on the test."

        3. Information-processing control

           Definition: statements indicating student efforts to engage in parsimony of information processing and to apply stop rules for information processing: specifically, efforts to quickly assess steps needed to perform a task and get down to business, efforts to avoid using strategies that overtax the information-processing system, or efforts to elect a time-out from the task for a brief period as a way of regrouping and refreshing themselves

           Example: "If I'm really tired, then the first thing I would think of is getting maybe an hour or two of sleep and then go to [the task], because then I'm able to concentrate better."

    B. Emotion control: managing the affective aspects of a task

        Definition: statements indicating student efforts to manage the affective aspects of a task and to control potentially debilitating states of worry or anxiety

        Example: "And I said, 'Now, sit down, try to relax.'"

    C. Motivation control: managing the expectancy aspects of a task

        1. Incentive escalation

           Definition: statements indicating student efforts to focus on imagined or realistic positive or negative consequences, including self-reward or self-punishment

           Example: "I have to pass [the test]; if I don't pass it, I'm not going to pass the class. I'll probably have to repeat it again or get an F, which I don't want to go on my record."

        2. Attribution/self-reinforcement

           Definition: statements indicating student efforts to provide self-reinforcement and reassurance

           Example: "Sometimes I get it, and I congratulate myself."

Figure 5.1. *(continued)*

3. Self-instruction

Definition: statements indicating student efforts to "tell" themselves necessary acts or steps to accomplishing a task

Example: "Let's try to think about this."

II. Overt processes of self-control

A. Environmental control

1. Task control

Definition: statements indicating student efforts to streamline or simplify a task or to determine how and when a task is to be completed

Example: "[I] get all the necessary materials that I need: books, dictionary, whatever it takes."

2. Setting control

Definition: statements indicating student efforts to determine or arrange where a task is to be completed

Example: "I'll try to get in a quiet place by myself."

B. Control of others in the task situation

1. Peer control

Definition: statements indicating student efforts to use peers as resources or to arrange situations so that friends do not detract from educational goals

Example: "[I might ask] if she can get tickets another day, or [say], '... If you're my friend, you would understand that I can't go with you,' or you know, 'If you would like to take somebody else.'"

2. Teacher control/assistance

Definition: statements indicating student efforts to obtain special assistance from teachers

Example: "[I would] ask the teacher if I can do it another day."

were discussed first, following the hypothesis that these more concrete strategies are easier to learn and can be building blocks for the internal strategies.

The first session concerned the task situation—when and where students study and the necessary materials for effective, uninterrupted studying. The second session involved becoming aware of and developing strategies for managing distractions in the home environment. The third session concerned learning to monitor one's own attention during academic pursuits. The fourth session involved maintaining a suitable state of mind for learning by controlling one's attention, negative emotions, and self-defeating motivational patterns. (A forty-page outline and supplementary materials describing this intervention are available from Trawick, who conducted a formal evaluation of this program; see Trawick, 1990.)

Procedures. The techniques used to present the volitional enhancement program include:

Instructional presentations, exercises, and activities to stimulate discussion and elicit students' thoughts about volitional management and control of their academic efforts in class and during homework.

Self-monitoring (record keeping) to enhance awareness of study behavior.

Student-developed positive self-statements that students could repeat prior to, during, and following specific academic situations to cope with self-defeating thoughts and behavior and to encourage themselves.

Modeling and role-playing of coping strategies.

Feedback from the instructor and from students' peers on assignments.

Session One: Control of Task and Setting. The first session taught students the overt strategies for task and setting control (see Figure 5.1). In very concrete ways, we focused on the optimal times to study, the characteristics of an appropriate place to study, and what materials must be at hand prior to the implementation of other, more traditional, study skills. This topic recognized that many urban community college students live in noisy and unspacious environments in which it is often hard to study and in which appropriate study conditions are difficult to create. Students reported, for example, that the volume of distractions they encountered in trying to study at home was considerable and that they were not always aware of how ineffective it is to study when other activities occur at the same time.

To prompt consideration of the importance of establishing an appropriate study environment, we discussed characteristics of the places in which students were currently studying. The focus was on concrete characteristics and conditions, such as noise level, temperature, and light. Also, we pointed out that conditions within the students themselves, such as tiredness, thirst, hunger, or comfort, may impact effective study. New thoughts and alternative strategies often then emerge in discussion, and many of these can be implemented in students' lives. Such strategies include taking a short nap before starting to study when one is too tired to study effectively at the moment; not eating a heavy meal before studying because it tends to make one sleepy; rearranging a study schedule to include going to the library after classes rather than going home; and enlisting baby-sitting trade-offs with new college friends to establish effective extended study periods.

Real-life constraints require further exploration and examination. It may be impossible to find an ideal study place, since the characteristics of this place are an individual matter, and spirited discussions often ensue regarding what constitutes an ideal study place. (For example, does music assist or distract students? If it assists, what kind of music, if any, might at least limit the potential for distraction from studying?) The discussions enable students to better specify the conditions over which they have control that may promote academic performance and to acquire new alternatives for establishing effective study conditions. Students are taught to be responsible not only for noticing whether they are in a conducive environment for study but also for getting themselves into such an environment.

Session Two: Control of Others in the Task Situation. The second session taught students strategies for controlling other people in their lives (see Figure 5.1). It addressed students' need to garner support from the significant others in their lives—their children, parents, friends, and other loved ones. For many students, the idea of going to college is a relatively recent one, and the influence of friends and loved ones must be examined explicitly in the context of the new life possibilities they see for themselves and their families. Research has documented the discontinuity that sometimes exists between the home and school environments of many urban community college students, particularly regarding academic effort (Weis, 1985). Some students have revealed that they come to college to get away from their relatives and friends who do not support their educational strivings; in such cases, significant others function more as distractions than as sources of support. In addressing this topic, we tried to help students find ways to communicate to loved ones that the students' education is important, and to introduce students to strategies for keeping loved ones from distracting them. Students began an explicit examination of the extent to which relationships with loved ones must be preserved, even as they acquired the skills, habits, and attitudes that have the potential to give them independence from these loved ones over time.

To introduce this content, we presented students with situations in which they knew they had to study (for an exam or a project for example) but then received a social call from a friend saying that the correct answer on a radio program has resulted in free tickets to a "can't miss" entertainment opportunity. Students were then asked to list the responses they could make to this "best friend" to express their renewed conviction to implement their intended plans to study. These statements were shared with group members with the goal of developing new alternatives: asking, for example, "Is it truly imperative for you even to answer the telephone?" Students then practiced their scenarios in small groups and received feedback from their peers and the instructor.

Session Three: Self-Monitoring to Control Attention. Session three taught the strategy of self-monitoring (see Figure 5.1) as a technique for remaining on task during academic work. The session was designed to raise students' awareness of lapses in concentration during academic tasks. To prompt awareness of their personal experiences of "mind-wandering" or daydreaming, students shared instances when they had been reading an academic assignment and suddenly stopped because they realized they were unaware of the previous content. Self-monitoring was then described as a way to keep concentration high by recognizing when other thoughts were intruding. These internal distracting thoughts, including competing academic and personal responsibilities, were compared to the external distractions (outside noises, poor lighting, social invitations, and so on) discussed in the first and second sessions.

Distracting thoughts students had experienced in the recent past were placed on the blackboard with the goal of demonstrating the notion that some distracting thoughts must be handled immediately for successful study to occur (for example, calling a doctor for the results of a child's x-ray), that other thoughts may be handled through time-management procedures (for examples, making up shopping lists and setting aside specific time for shopping), and that a great deal of time is wasted because of mind-wandering. The discussion and activities were summarized by pointing out that it is necessary for students to learn as much as possible about a situation they desire to change.

A self-monitoring assignment was introduced as a way for students to begin to practice becoming aware of their thoughts during study—to "watch" themselves—in preparation for learning a technique in the next session to control these thoughts. In the self-monitoring assignment, students were asked to keep a record sheet beside them as they worked and to place a tally on the sheet each time a distracting thought interfered with ongoing study efforts, to categorize the thoughts at the end of the study session, and to indicate what they learned about their study patterns.

Session Four: Motivational Control. Session four taught the covert strategies for controlling students' attention, negative emotions, and self-defeating motivational patterns (see Figure 5.1). This involved showing students how to recover from lapses in attention and to turn negative, self-defeating emotions and motivational patterns ("I'll never understand this material") into positive ones ("I'll succeed if I just do my work every day"). A strategy that has been called, from various perspectives, self-verbalization (Meichenbaum, 1972), positive self-talk, and internal dialogue (Vygotsky, 1962) was used to introduce the fourth session. This strategy, which we called self-coaching (Collins and others, 1981), was intended to help students learn to control their personal resources of attention, concentration, and motivation.

One self-coaching activity used the example of a baseball game. In a situation in which all attention is riveted on the pitcher and batter in the ninth inning of a tied ball game, there is a great deal of noise that could be expected to distract them both. Also, athletes know that they do not always hit home runs and that they cannot allow one bad playing error to ruin the rest of their efforts. Like athletes in these situations, students can *learn* to use positive self-coaching to control their attention and emotions and to stay motivated to reach their goals. Students indicated the kinds of thoughts they have experienced when an assignment was very difficult or very dull or when they had performed poorly on an examination. Having positive self-statements or "scripts" ready in advance was suggested as helpful for various situations, including, for example, controlling attention during study sessions, concentrating when studies are dull or when it would be more enjoyable to be out with friends, and handling emotions when a low examination grade is received.

Students were then asked to develop personally meaningful positive self-statements that would motivate them when their academic responsibilities seemed overwhelming: for example, prior to or during an examination or a presentation when they suddenly realized the importance of the endeavor or when anxiety threatened to unnerve them. A few statements written by the approximately sixty urban community college students who have completed the volitional enhancement program indicate their personal struggles: "If I don't get my work done now, I'll end up a bum." "I have to study hard so I can be a model mother to my daughter." "I have to prepare for exams way in advance to avoid being anxious." These personal statements were not openly shared; instead, students were encouraged to keep them on 3 x 5 cards and to use the cards as anchors when academic requirements seemed overwhelming, when their concentration dropped, or when anxiety threatened to disrupt intended academic plans.

Student Comments

As part of the formal evaluation of this program, a semistructured interview was administered to ten students to elicit their comments and reactions. More than half reported that participation in the program represented the first time in their academic careers that they had given real thought to the process of applying effort towards schoolwork and studying. One student, J.B., was typical in making this response: "I never really realized how I was studying or even thought about how I was studying. . . . I would just study. [I never thought about] where I was studying, how much noise— . . . so it helped me a lot."

Other students indicated that prior to the program, they had been aware that there were relatively more and less efficient ways to study but that they had never made it a point to put these methods into practice. For example, M.S. said: "You know the habits and everything; you know them, but you're just—you're not conscious of them, and you're not putting them into practice or anything. . . . So you're not . . . using them as a tool."

Of the ten students interviewed, eight spontaneously mentioned that the most important changes resulting from the program were concerned with gaining control over their study environment. One example of the concrete nature of the changes students attributed to the program is that five of the ten students interviewed stated that they had made changes in handling distractions from siblings, friends, and spouses. R.M. stated:

> One of the most helpful things was to remind myself how to deal with certain situations. For example, . . . I have told my friends that I am in school, but . . . I did that without thinking in the future, you know. And now I have the fresh idea in my mind why I did that, . . . so I can now have an answer more easily than before. . . . Probably if somebody calls, maybe to invite me to a concert, I can be very clear—I mean, not being rude or anything like that, but I can be very clear. I can get to the point and try just to switch that situation to something different, . . . for example, to invite them to do something the next day as an alternative.

A more covert focus that these students commented on was training in the use of self-coaching strategies. Six of the ten students made reference to the work done on self-coaching as a way of "disciplining" themselves to study. J.S. felt that instruction in self-coaching was the most important part of the intervention:

> I learned to tell myself that my education is more important than anything else. . . . So you know that you have this goal that you have to reach, and you know that . . . unless you try you won't get it. There are times when . . . I'm thinking about something else or I don't feel good . . . but I know that I have to [study] because that time is precious. I say, "If you miss it, that's it. It won't come back." And I say, "Let's go back [and study]." I know that I have to do it, and I learned to tell myself, this is important, and I'm going to do it now.

L.W. said that she learned to coach herself by reminding herself of the long-term benefits to be gained by studying now.

> I need to do better, . . . to look for the long term instead of the short term, where I want to be . . . a few years from now. . . . I have been in school before. This is my second opportunity. I want to make the best of my second chance. I'm more mature now, so I . . . just keep telling myself, "You're doing this for your best benefit in the long run.". . . Being out in the workforce, not having a college degree, you gotta stay at a certain place, and I don't want to stay there. I want to go above . . . thinking of my goals and self-coaching myself to go on for what I really want.

These comments indicate that urban community college students can be made increasingly knowledgeable about appropriate study environments and useful strategies for handling distractions as well as about self-monitoring and self-coaching with a short-term intensive volitional enhancement experience.

Program Issues and Perspectives

The kind of content used in the volitional enhancement program acknowledges that many urban community college students may be introduced to new possibilities not focal in their present reality. We are attempting to teach new behaviors, skills, and attitudes. The notion of who a student *could* become is central here. Students may have had limited access to or contact with models in their environment who routinely demonstrate the needed characteristics. Nonetheless, urban community college students can be led to draw upon the resources that they do have related to achievement opportunities and strivings (Cole and Scribner, 1974). This type of volitional enhancement program may be viewed as providing a competing environmental model for students whose current environments may not lend themselves to initiating or supporting particular models of learning and behavior. The program focuses on students' needs to change their existing thoughts and behavior as well as on giving them specific new knowledge and thoughts (for example, the idea that they can formally monitor study time).

In keeping with the social-constructivist theory that provided the framework for the implementation of our program, it is important to remember that changing student thinking and behavior is a complex undertaking. Individual change occurs through a gradual process of internalizing knowledge over a period of time. Accordingly, a program that is longer in duration than four weeks, with shorter amounts of time per session and incorporated on a regular basis into the college curriculum, ought to facilitate specific self-management outcomes. The program process requires students to perceive themselves differently, to acquire a view of themselves as individuals who engage in volitional and self-management strategies and who follow through on schoolwork. As educators, we must acknowledge that it is easier for people to behave in comfortable, familiar ways than to change and that learning to stay engaged for long periods of time in the study endeavor will take time.

Moreover, it is important for us to remember that learning involves making errors. It is important for us, as professionals, to examine our view of error. We know from research that errors help students learn where to focus their academic effort (Dweck, 1986). Errors serve to specify the knowledge one already has as well as the knowledge and skills one has not yet mastered. But from students' perspective, an important concern at this stage in their academic careers may be to avoid the appearance of failure (Covington, 1985). Thus, for example, such behavior as ignoring errors, procrastinating, and setting unrealistic goals may be ways that students protect their own sense of self-worth. If one appears not to try, then it is *not possible* to fail (see Chapter Four).

Instructors need to assess the extent to which urban community college students have been appropriately prepared for instructional environments in which errors are viewed as a natural and normal part of the learning process. It seems important for students to learn to cope with errors and skillfully handle the negative feelings that accompany them. Similarly, opportunities that encourage students to access their own thinking processes (investigating, for example, *how* they choose response options on homework exercises or *how* they eliminate other response choices) help students become accustomed to thinking about their thinking.

Faculty development programs for college instructors might profitably incorporate instruction in such volitional process skills rather than focusing narrowly on instruction in content alone. This is consistent with other strategy-training research (for example, Pressley, Borkowski, and O'Sullivan, 1984), which suggests that durable strategy use requires an explicit connection between the instructional situation and the usefulness of the strategy. In the meantime, the difficulties that urban community college students display in the area of academic volitional control may help to explain the frustration experienced by teachers and students alike when their joint efforts are unsuccessful. These difficulties may explain how teachers can be correct in saying,

"I taught it" and students correct in saying, "I studied it," even after students are unable to demonstrate gains in learning on achievement tests. It is not that the students lack effort or "will." Their tenacious efforts to remain in school suggest otherwise. Rather, they may need to fine-tune their volitional resources to benefit from their prodigious efforts in the face of so many environmental and personal distractions.

References

Alkin, M. C. (ed.). *Encyclopedia of Educational Research.* Vol. 1. New York: Macmillan, 1992.

American Association of Community Colleges. *Community Colleges: A National Profile.* Washington, D.C.: American Association of Community Colleges, 1993.

Bandura, A. "Self-Efficacy: Toward a Unifying Theory of Behavioral Change." *Psychological Review,* 1977, *84,* 191–215.

Bandura, A. *Social Foundations of Thought and Action: A Social Cognitive Theory.* Englewood Cliffs, N.J.: Prentice Hall, 1986.

Cole, M., and Scribner, S. *Culture and Thought.* New York: Wiley, 1974.

Collins, K. W., Dansereau, D. F., Garland, J. C., Holley, C. D., and McDonald, B. A. "Control of Concentration During Academic Tasks." *Journal of Educational Psychology,* 1981, *73,* 122–128.

Corno, L. "Self-Regulated Learning: A Volitional Analysis." In B. J. Zimmerman and D. H. Schunk (eds.), *Self-Regulated Learning and Academic Achievement: Theory, Research, and Practice.* New York: Springer-Verlag, 1989a.

Corno, L. "What It Means to Be Literate About Classrooms." In D. Bloome (ed.), *Classrooms and Literacy.* Norwood, N.J.: Ablex, 1989b.

Corno, L. "The Best-Laid Plans: Modern Conceptions of Volition and Educational Research." *Educational Researcher,* 1993, *22,* 14–22.

Corno, L., and Kanfer, R. "The Role of Volition in Learning and Performance." In L. Darling-Hammond (ed.), *Review of Research in Education.* Washington, D.C.: American Educational Research Association, 1993.

Covington, M. V. "The Motive for Self-Worth." In C. Ames and R. Ames (eds.), *Research on Motivation in Education: Student Motivation.* San Diego: Academic Press, 1985.

Cross, K. P. *Accent on Learning: Improving Instruction and Reshaping the Curriculum.* San Francisco: Jossey-Bass, 1976.

Dole, J., Duffy, G., Roehler, L., and Pearson, P. D. "Moving from the Old to the New: Research on Reading Comprehension Instruction." *Review of Research in Education,* 1991, *61,* 239–264.

Dweck, C. "Motivational Processes Affecting Learning." *American Psychologist,* 1986, *41,* 1040–1048.

Kuhl, J. "Volitional Mediators of Cognition-Behavior Consistency: Self-Regulatory Processes and Action Versus State Orientation." In J. Kuhl and J. Beckmann (eds.), *Action Control: From Cognition to Behavior.* New York: Springer-Verlag, 1985.

Meichenbaum, D. "Cognitive Modification of Test-Anxious College Students." *Journal of Consulting and Clinical Psychology,* 1972, *39,* 370–380.

Meichenbaum, D. *Cognitive Behavior Modification.* New York: Plenum, 1977.

Paris, S. G., and Winograd, P. "How Metacognition Can Promote Academic Learning and Instruction." In B. F. Jones and L. Idol (eds.), *Dimensions of Thinking and Cognitive Instruction.* Vol. 1. Hillsdale, N.J.: Erlbaum, 1990.

Pintrich, P. R. "Implications of Psychological Research on Student Learning and College Teaching for Teacher Education." In W. R. Houston (ed.), *Handbook of Research on Teacher Education.* New York: Macmillan, 1990.

Pintrich, P. R., and De Groot, E. "Motivational and Self-Regulated Learning Components of Classroom Academic Performance." *Journal of Educational Psychology,* 1990, *82,* 33–40.

Pressley, M., Borkowski, J. G., and O'Sullivan, J. T. "Memory Strategy Instruction Is Made of This: Metamemory and Durable Strategy Use." *Educational Psychology,* 1984, *19,* 94–107.

Pressley, M., Borkowski, J. G., and Schneider, W. "Good Information Processing: What It Is and How Education Can Promote It." *International Journal of Educational Research,* 1989, *13,* 857–867.

Pressley, M., and Levin, J. R. (eds.). *Cognitive Strategy Research: Psychological Foundations.* New York: Springer-Verlag, 1983.

Schunk, D. H. *Learning Theories: An Educational Perspective.* New York: Merrill, 1991.

Schunk, D. H., and Zimmerman, B. J. (eds.). *Self-Regulation of Learning and Performance: Issues and Educational Applications.* Hillsdale, N.J.: Erlbaum, 1994.

Shapiro, L. "Effects of Written Metacognitive and Cognitive Strategy Instruction on the Elementary Algebra Achievement of College Students in a Remedial Mathematics Course." Unpublished doctoral dissertation, Teachers College, Columbia University, 1988.

Trawick, L. "Effects of a Cognitive-Behavioral Intervention on the Motivation, Volition, and Achievement of Academically Underprepared College Students." Unpublished doctoral dissertation, Teachers College, Columbia University, 1990.

Vygotsky, L. S. *Thought and Language.* New York: Wiley, 1962.

Weinstein, C. E., and Mayer, R. F. "The Teaching of Learning Strategies." In M. C. Wittrock (ed.), *Handbook of Research on Teaching.* (3rd ed.) New York: Macmillan, 1986.

Weinstein, C. E., and Underwood, V. L. "Learning Strategies: The How of Learning." In J. Segal, S. Chipman, and R. Glaser (eds.), *Relating Instruction to Basic Research.* Hillsdale, N.J.: Erlbaum, 1985.

Weis, L. *Between Two Worlds: Black Students in an Urban Community College.* New York: Routledge & Kegan Paul, 1985.

Zimmerman, B. J. "Models of Self-Regulated Learning and Academic Achievement." In B. J. Zimmerman and D. H. Schunk (eds.), *Self-Regulated Learning and Academic Achievement: Theory, Research, and Practice.* New York: Springer-Verlag, 1989.

Zimmerman, B. J., and Martinez-Pons, M. "Construct Validation of a Strategy Model of Student Self-Regulated Learning." *Journal of Educational Psychology,* 1988, *80,* 284–290.

Zimmerman, B. J., and Schunk, D. H. (eds.). *Self-Regulated Learning and Academic Achievement: Theory, Research, and Practice.* New York: Springer-Verlag, 1989.

LAVERGNE TRAWICK is associate professor in the counseling department at LaGuardia Community College, City University of New York.

LYN CORNO is professor of education and psychology at Teachers College, Columbia University.

One part of a faculty development program that is based on the classroom research movement focuses on how faculty can use the research and methodological tools relating to student motivation and self-regulation in research in their own classroom.

College Faculty as Educational Researchers: Discipline-Focused Studies of Student Motivation and Self-Regulated Learning

Stuart A. Karabenick, Jan Collins-Eaglin

Many colleges and universities have programs to enhance instructional effectiveness by increasing faculty awareness of beneficial teaching practices. Increasingly, these recommendations are based on the premise that students learn best when they are self-regulated and actively involved in the learning process. However, faculty development techniques designed to encourage faculty to promote active student learning are themselves often passive and brief (for example, newsletters, seminars, or speakers) and do not model the prescription. Instructional effectiveness with faculty, as with students, is more likely when they are engaged in long-term, sustained instruction (Weimer, 1990). An activity that meets these criteria is faculty-initiated research on teaching and learning.

By designing, executing, and communicating the results of their own studies, faculty can achieve greater insight into the teaching-learning process, understand at a more fundamental level the instructional and curricular implications of others' research, and enhance their own instructional expertise. In this chapter, we begin by reviewing efforts to promote faculty research on teaching and learning at the classroom level. We then describe a new development program that emphasizes grounding faculty research on postsecondary teaching and learning within a comprehensive theoretical and empirical framework that includes a focus on active student involvement and self-regulatory processes.

The impressive success of the classroom research movement was facilitated in large measure by Angelo and Cross's systematic presentation of classroom assessment techniques (CATs) (1993). The popularity of classroom research demonstrates considerable faculty interest in an active, empirical approach to instructional improvement, at least when that research addresses specific classroom issues (for example, determining what students have gleaned from a lecture) and requires minimal research design skills or theoretical background. Cross and Angelo promote the use of CATs primarily for studies of specific learning situations, speculating that, with the exception of instructors in the social sciences, most faculty have neither the desire nor the time to expand beyond classroom research in order to engage in traditional educational research. As Angelo and Cross state explicitly, "It is not our desire to turn a dedicated chemistry teacher into an educational researcher who conducts research on learning in chemistry classrooms" (1993, p. 385). This position is understandable from a classroom research perspective. Considering most discipline-oriented and specialized academic career paths, it seems unlikely that faculty would be interested in expending their professional time and energy on studying college teaching and student cognition and motivation. Even if faculty were interested, institutional incentives are generally not favorable, as most departments and colleges would consider such activity unimportant, counting little or not at all toward merit, tenure, or promotion (Boyer, 1990).

However, there are also reasons why faculty might undertake such research. Boyer also notes that senior faculty often seek new challenges that are integrative and applied, including how to communicate their disciplinary knowledge more effectively to their students. Younger faculty may consider classroom research to be a way to demonstrate their commitment to instructional excellence. Such research is also a next step for those who have exhausted most other development program options. Our experience at a large comprehensive university suggests many such faculty do exist. They consider the opportunity not only attractive but intellectually stimulating and an important facet of their careers.

The question is how to address the needs of those who wish to conduct their own applied and generalizable discovery-oriented research on teaching, student motivation, and learning. First, many will need to acquire additional research design (quantitative and/or qualitative) and/or statistical skills. The Harvard Assessment Seminars (Light, 1990, 1992) are excellent models for developing the skills that would equip faculty to undertake a variety of institutional research and evaluation studies. We believe, however, that such programs should also include a background of theory and research in postsecondary teaching and learning, specifically the motivational, cognitive, and self-regulating determinants of college student performance.

A Program of Discipline-Focused Educational Research

The ongoing Research on Teaching and Learning (RTL) program at our comprehensive university is designed to provide faculty with that comprehensive background in the process of designing and conducting what we term *discipline-focused educational research*. Program participation begins with an intensive seminar that examines theoretical approaches to and research on postsecondary teaching and learning and basic quantitative and qualitative research design concepts.[1] Primary emphasis is placed upon student cognition, motivation, and self-regulation. Faculty then design, conduct, and communicate the results of studies within their own disciplines that contextualize general theoretical and research design principles.

Program Participants. The number and the characteristics of applicants to our program support our belief that faculty are interested in empirical studies of teaching and learning.[2] Applicants to date vary considerably by experience (one to thirty years), discipline, and research expertise. Many have participated in other developmental activities and view positively the prospect of gaining a more in-depth understanding of the teaching-learning process. Several have expressed a desire to work with colleagues in different disciplines who share their interest in teaching and learning.

Interest in the teaching and learning process—as evidenced by activities such as the use of CATs and other attempts to explore the effects of instruction-related classroom variables—is the most important criterion used to select faculty for participation. Research expertise, however, is not considered essential. Although selecting faculty with greater research skills would probably increase the likelihood, as well as the quality, of studies emerging from the program, it would eliminate an important segment of the faculty population. Rather, the approach is eclectic with respect to prior research experience, striving as much as possible to include a broad range of expertise.[3]

Typical of junior faculty, one assistant professor had attended several development workshops; read articles about college teaching, critical thinking, and problem solving; and was particularly concerned about creating a positive learning environment and establishing herself as an effective instructor. Another had experimented with classroom research and had informally compared cooperative and individualistic learning structures. That experience spurred her interest in a more scholarly approach to postsecondary teaching and learning. A third stated a desire to investigate what motivates students to engage in self-regulated learning activities and classroom discussion. Senior faculty were similar to their junior colleagues with the exception that they were more likely to have established disciplinary research or scholarly careers.

Participants' research backgrounds reflect the diversity that exists at many comprehensive universities. Many have not engaged in research after their dissertations. Some are productive in their fields, but their activity (for example, political science or English) does not include empirical research. Others (for example, in psychology and biology) have considerable research expertise but have not applied their skills to teaching and learning issues. A few have conducted research on teaching and learning but not in higher education. The most experienced have published in the area of instructional technology.

Program Seminar. Participants' first experience with the program consists of an in-depth research seminar that provides the coherent conceptual framework that is absent when, for example, faculty are given mini-grants to pursue studies on their own. Based on a comprehensive review by McKeachie and others (1990) the approach (presented schematically in Figure 6.1) emphasizes motivational and cognitive mediators of student learning. It assumes that these mediators are influenced by instructional methods and task requirements and that they affect student involvement in the learning process and student self-regulation, which, in turn, affect student achievement.

Beginning seminar discussions review research on teaching in higher education, focusing on such topics as class size, lecture versus discussion, peer and cooperative learning, and the evaluation of teaching (see, for example, McKeachie, 1990). Examples of student entry characteristics examined include theories of intelligence (for example, fluid and crystallized intelligence, Gardner's multiple intelligences, and Sternberg's triarchic theory); personality (relatively stable individual differences) as exemplified by motivational style and test anxiety; and cognitive style (for example, field independence/dependence and surface versus deep processing). Consideration is given to the value of typologies (such as Myers-Briggs) in understanding the dynamic and self-regulatory nature of student learning.

Cognition is discussed next, including how knowledge is structured in different disciplines (Donald, 1983, 1990) and what students' cognitive structures are. To aid their understanding of cognitive structures, faculty complete an ordered-tree exercise (Naveh-Benjamin, McKeachie, Lin, and Tucker, 1986; Reitman and Reuter, 1980) that requires ordering a set of concepts (for example, quantitative and qualitative research design principles) according to their similarity. They also complete a "fill-in" that assesses how well missing concepts can be inserted into an existing structure (Naveh-Benjamin and Lin, 1988, 1989). Additional material covered includes student problem solving and critical thinking.

Once faculty have a greater understanding of cognitive structures, focus shifts to how student achievement depends on the effectiveness of self-regulation, that is, the use of cognitive, metacognitive, and resource-management strategies (McKeachie and others, 1990; Weinstein and Mayer, 1986). Cognitive strategies are the ways students process (that is, attend to, encode, store, and recall) information required by instructional tasks. These strategies include rehearsal, organization, elaboration (establishing links between concepts), and critical thinking. Students' ability to regulate cognitive strategies depends on their use of metacognitive strategies that include planning and monitoring. Resource-management strategies include arranging of time and study environments, knowing how much effort to exert and when to exert it

Figure 6.1. General Model of College Teaching and Learning

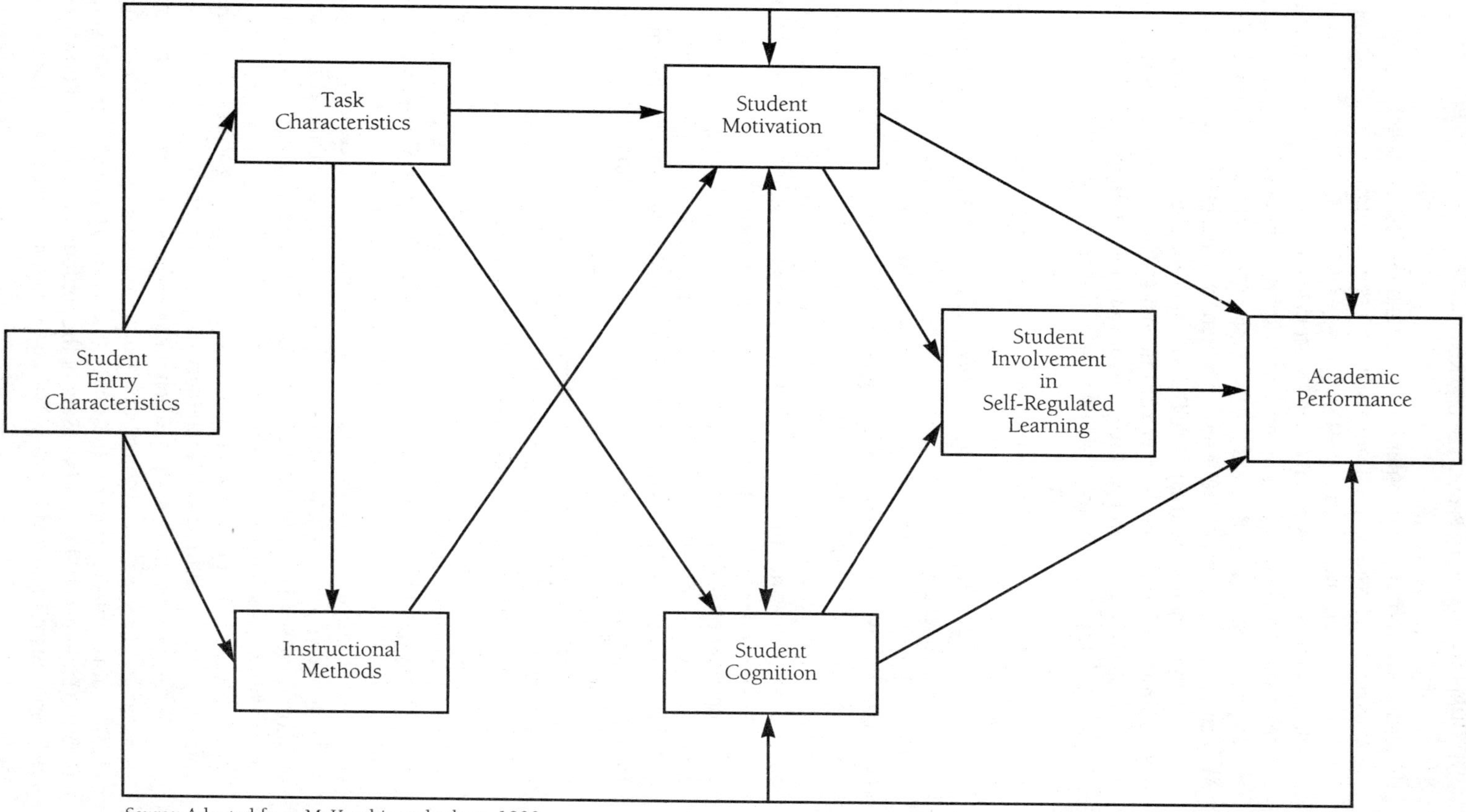

Source: Adapted from McKeachie and others, 1990.

(for example, learning how to persist at less than interesting tasks), and seeking assistance and asking questions when necessary (Karabenick and Knapp, 1991; Karabenick and Sharma, 1994).

According to the approach taken by McKeachie and his colleagues, student motivation is determined by students' expectations of success, including self-efficacy (Bandura, 1982) and the value placed on achievement outcomes. Motivation is a function of the extent to which students believe they are capable of attaining their goals (that is, self-efficacious) and the degree to which the setting promotes behavior-outcome contingencies. The importance of student attributions for success and failure (see, for example, Weiner, 1979, 1986) is presented in this context. Intrinsic interest in the course material, its importance to the students, its utility for the students' futures, and students' mastery versus performance goal orientations (see, for example, Ames, 1992) are also discussed.

Participants examine how these concepts are operationalized by examining and completing the Motivated Strategies for Learning Questionnaire (MSLQ) (Pintrich, Smith, Garcia, and McKeachie, 1993), which they are encouraged to use in their classes, along with a companion monograph (Johnson and others, 1991) that provides suggestions ("teaching tips"). For example, having students select their own paper or presentation topics is suggested as a way of increasing students' control beliefs (that is, beliefs that behavior is related to outcomes). When more than one way of measuring concepts is available, the additional ways are introduced. In the case of learning strategies, an additional way of measuring is the Learning and Study Strategies Inventory (LASSI) (Weinstein, Palmer, and Schulte, 1987). Relevant original source materials (typically journal articles) are included wherever possible. For example, faculty members review Weinstein and Mayer (1986) and Weinstein, Zimmerman, and Palmer (1988) in conjunction with learning strategies. The discussion of student thinking and cognitive processes includes Wittrock's review (1986) and Donald's work (1983, 1990) on knowledge structures.

Research Design. Participants examine and contrast positivistic (Light, Singer, and Willett, 1990) and nonpositivistic (qualitative) research assumptions and design principles (see, for example, Marshall and Rossman, 1989; Patton, 1987). Quantitative topics include the proper framing of research questions, sampling, measurement, statistical and experimental control, internal and external validity, correlation, regression, main and interaction effects, and structural modeling. Basic statistical topics of hypothesis testing such as type I error, power, and variance accounted for are included. Qualitative research topics discussed include site selection, cover stories, gaining access, researcher roles, rapport and subjectivity, and interviewing techniques.

Additional Content. Faculty participants also contribute relevant resource material. In one session, an interest in learning styles, for example, led to a discussion of recent evidence on the utility of the Myers-Briggs Type Indicator (MBTI) (Pittenger, 1993). A discussion of the confounding of prior knowledge and topic interest resulted in our providing participants with Tobias's excellent review (1994) of this issue. Participants are also introduced to several research-related resources. This includes apprising them of periodicals on college teaching in their fields (see Cashin and Clegg, 1993). Those who are unacquainted with research databases are introduced to CD-ROM versions of PsychLit and ERIC.

Seminar Research. Participants gain experience with design, data management, and statistical issues in the process of conducting campuswide descriptive-correlational studies. For example, one project assessed student and faculty perceptions of the goal orientations (mastery versus performance) and incentive structures (individualistic, competitive, or cooperative) of their classes (Collins-Eaglin and Karabenick, 1994); another examined the degree to which students and faculty believe they are "responsible" for a variety of instructional outcomes, such as maintaining student motivation and relating the course material to other knowledge students may have (Karabenick and Collins-Eaglin, 1995). The studies represent many of the participants' first empirical research experiences, and with few exceptions, their first contact with education-related research.

Seminar Process. The seminar is designed to be highly interactive and participatory. Typical interactions alternate between discussions of general principles and discipline-specific issues. The process of relating personal experiences to general principles enhances participants' understanding of the theoretical approach and the empirical literature. Faculty have reported that exposure to how their colleagues interpret and apply concepts tends to deepen their own level of understanding, which underscores the importance of multidisciplinary seminar membership. As might be expected, there is more frequent mention of general principles of student motivation and self-regulated learning, including how these principles relate to faculty members' own discipline-focused research projects, as the seminar progresses.

Faculty Research

Faculty culminate seminar participation by designing discipline-related studies. This stage requires that research questions be articulated along with appropriate design strategies to address them. Design modifications are typically necessary once faculty confront the constraints of data collection within a university environment (for example, obtaining cooperation from students and colleagues). Many faculty acquire computer-related skills during the data-management phase, and statistical testing and interpretation markedly enhance their understanding of concepts they have previously only discussed.

Reflecting the characteristics of educational research in general, most of the studies have been descriptive, correlational, or quasi-experimental; few have been truly experimental. Several have involved student motivation and self-regulation. They ranged from an intensive focus on one class to extensive surveys involving over one thousand students. A few studies could be classified as classically discovery-oriented educational research, some as evaluative or assessment oriented, and others had elements of both. Most important, however, is that virtually all have been discipline focused, that is, of direct relevance to faculty areas of expertise. Although space limitations preclude an exhaustive listing here, brief descriptions can be presented that exemplify the links between the studies and the program's overall theoretical approach, the diversity of faculty interests, and the theme of self-regulation. To date, some projects have been completed; others are in process or in the design stage. Results of several have been presented at professional conferences; results of others have been published or are in some phase of the submission process.

Psychology. Representing discipline-focused research grounded in theory was a project in which a clinical psychologist tested whether the relationship between general psychological distress and academic achievement is mediated by students' motivational tendencies and their use of strategic self-regulation. A structural equation-modeling approach provided support for indirect causal paths from students' experienced psychological distress to self-efficacy and resource-management strategies (directed at managing time, study environment, and effort), which were, in turn, causally linked to student grades. Evidence also suggested that students' use of cognitive and metacognitive strategies affected their regulation of effort, time, and study environment. In addition to their theoretical import, the results have implications for student counseling practices. The instructor is conducting further studies that examine the effects of specific dimensions of distress, such as depression, on academic performance.

Special Education. Theoretical and disciplinary linkage is also exemplified by the project of a program participant who assessed changes in preservice teachers' beliefs about learners with disabilities. The study focused on models of the helping relationship that include teachers' beliefs about learners' use of self-regulatory help-seeking behavior (Karabenick and Knapp, 1991; Newman, 1991) and about the locus of responsibility for their problems and solutions (Brickman, 1982). Several scenarios assessed the likelihood of certain teacher responses to students who have special needs in the classroom. Interest focused on a model predicated on the absence of students' responsibility for their conditions and the desirability of student empowerment, with teacher assistance, to overcome those conditions.

Accounting and Finance. A senior professor tested whether cooperative classroom activities and variations in individual and group performance incentives (see, for example, Slavin, 1983; Slavin and others, 1985) would affect student performance, motivation, and use of regulatory learning strategies in introductory accounting. Results suggested that not all cooperative classroom activities that replace traditional lecture improve student performance. The instructor found that whereas performance did not vary as a function of cooperative and incentive conditions, students were more likely to enjoy working cooperatively.

Mathematics, Communication, and Theater Arts. There is substantial evidence that anxiety disrupts student learning and decreases the use of regulatory strategies (see, for example, McCombs, 1988; Schmeck, 1988). An extensive survey by colleagues in math and communications compared retrospective reports of students' experiences with English and math during elementary and high schools to their anxiety in college math and speech courses. Also examined were students' conceptions of ability as stable or variable, their interest in course content, their idea of the utility of course content, their attributions for success and failure, and their self-efficacy. Results indicated there was less anxiety than anticipated in both speech and math and an absence of expected gender differences in all but developmental (that is, remedial) math courses.

Professional Development

As a result of the seminar and faculty research experiences, both formal evaluation (pre- and postseminar questionnaires for example) and spontaneous comments reveal a high degree of faculty enthusiasm for the program. It appears to be professionally stimulating and to reinforce and even rejuvenate faculty interest in discovering more about the learning process. Program impact is also assessed through journals, which not only serve as an ongoing evaluation of the seminar but also chronicle the development of faculty as they reflect on the learning, teaching, and research process. For example, when faculty were reading about student cognition and knowledge structures, one participant wrote that he typically was "concerned about the delivery of content, not how knowledge is obtained nor how to assess the process." Learning more about student cognition deepened his understanding of how students structure that content.

As they become more active in the process of studying the complexities of learning and academic performance, faculty increasingly perceive connections between their own teaching and the theoretical and empirical postsecondary literature. During the seminar, discussions of teaching techniques take place almost exclusively in the context of examining the empirical and theoretical literature. Faculty frequently state that the program provides them with greater insight into the rationale and underlying principles of instructional practices recommended to them. Their increased sophistication also creates greater awareness of the limitations of research and provides the impetus for them to comprehensively analyze the empirical basis for conclusions and recommendations for improving student learning.

Faculty with little design and statistical knowledge or familiarity with the concepts and theories have expressed apprehension during the initial phases of the seminar. As might be expected, they become more comfortable over time. Faculty with extensive research experience find the seminar equally beneficial. One who taught learning English as a second language commented that "the material presented has complemented my work and research in applied linguistics/psycholinguistics. Listening to others' research areas is helping me expand my own research and also realize that my research complements that done by educators across a wide range of content domains and may shed light on the theoretical and practical implications of [schema] theory."

Although knowledge gains have not been assessed directly, one of the seminar activities provided evidence of change. As noted, the discussion of research on students' knowledge structures includes an exercise using a technique called an ordered tree (Naveh-Benjamin and Lin, 1991). An algorithm that uses both consistency and distance information generates an inferred knowledge structure. Figure 6.2 presents one participant's ordered tree of statistical and research design concepts as it was drawn at the beginning of the seminar (the upper tree) and at the end (the lower tree). The first tree shows very little structure, that is, only a few concepts are systematically related. The postseminar structure, which is much more articulated and hierarchical, although not totally "accurate," illustrates an increased understanding of the relationship between the concepts. We can infer, for example, that the faculty member construed as related several terms concerned with sampling (differential selection, probability sample, stratified sample, and random assignment).

Institutional Impact

Programs such as Research on Teaching and Learning have the potential to shape the discussion of teaching and learning and to influence the instructional climate, shifting the perspective from individuals to the broader university culture. When there are an increased number of faculty who have an appropriate knowledge base and who conduct research using constructs such as self-regulation, knowledge structures, and comprehension monitoring, these instructors can promote a more meaningful discourse than would otherwise occur. Moreover, institutional support and recognition for this type of program have the effect of legitimizing faculty research on teaching and learning (Boyer, 1990).

On a departmental level, faculty research in the content area may have direct effects on instruction and curriculum. The RTL program, for example, sponsors presentations that allow faculty the opportunity to present the results of their investigations, stressing instructional and curricular implications pertinent for their own departments. There has been exceptional receptivity to these presentations due to the degree of scholarship and theoretical rationale underlying the studies, and the studies often result in significant curricular changes. For example, the results of a special education instructor's study prompted the department to alter the way an introductory course is taught to several hundred students. Above and beyond the departmental presentations, the program also sponsors campuswide sessions that provide an opportunity for wider dissemination of participants' research to faculty from other disciplines.

Campuswide studies that focus on various aspects of general student learning and use of self-regulated learning strategies as opposed to specific

Figure 6.2. Faculty Participant's Cognitive Tree Structures for Research Design Concepts

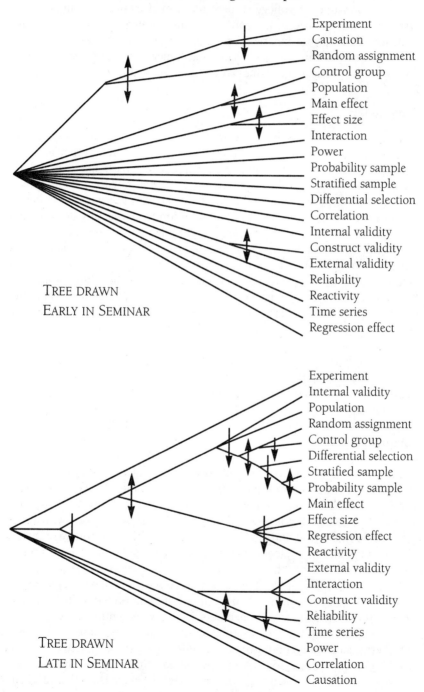

Experiment
Causation
Random assignment
Control group
Population
Main effect
Effect size
Interaction
Power
Probability sample
Stratified sample
Differential selection
Correlation
Internal validity
Construct validity
External validity
Reliability
Reactivity
Time series
Regression effect

TREE DRAWN
EARLY IN SEMINAR

Experiment
Internal validity
Population
Random assignment
Control group
Differential selection
Stratified sample
Probability sample
Main effect
Effect size
Regression effect
Reactivity
External validity
Interaction
Construct validity
Reliability
Time series
Power
Correlation
Causation

TREE DRAWN
LATE IN SEMINAR

disciplinary studies also contribute to the program's institutional impact. For example, program surveys have focused on student and faculty beliefs about who is responsible for college student performance, and on comparison of first-year students' use of regulatory learning strategies in structured and unstructured first-year experience programs. Results of the research are distributed to faculty through a series of nontechnical research reports that raise theoretical and pedagogical issues and help create dialogue.

Conclusion

Our experience suggests that there are indeed faculty who are motivated and willing to engage in discipline-focused educational research, if they are given the appropriate time and support. As several faculty participants noted, the program has the potential to affect significantly not only their own teaching but also their departments and the university. There is every reason to believe that our model could be an important addition to any faculty development program. The degree to which it is generalizable depends on such factors as institution size and mission. Large comprehensive universities, such as ours, would seem most suitable because of their emphasis on both teaching and research. Smaller liberal arts colleges that focus on teaching are also likely to have interested faculty engage in research that would complement their instructional emphasis. However, the program may not be as successful at research universities that stress discipline-based research and scholarship almost exclusively.

Certainly the program that we describe here could be considered ambitious, both in the number of faculty supported at a given time and the range of activities undertaken (the seminar itself, campuswide studies, individual faculty research projects, and communication of results).[4] It would, for example, be possible to forgo, or to at least limit, the campuswide study, which requires considerable time and effort. Limiting the program's scope would also be tenable, through such steps as reducing the number of faculty participants (although too few participants would decrease the likelihood of interdisciplinary synergy, which is an important process outcome). However, whatever modifications are made and whatever elements are adopted or adapted, included or excluded, it is essential that participants be provided with a comprehensive theoretical and empirical background in postsecondary teaching and learning and in student motivation and self-regulation, using either the materials cited here or other appropriate sources. As noted, that content provides the foundation for worthwhile seminar discussion on which meaningful faculty research is built. It is also an important component of the scholarly activity that engenders faculty members' curiosity and enthusiasm.

We began with the premise that developmental programs that involve a long-term, sustained commitment are more likely to be effective (Weimer, 1990). Our experiences to date support this conclusion as we have witnessed the ways in which our faculty participants have developed. They have a better understanding of the theoretical and empirical basis for instructional practices and a deeper appreciation of the research process, both in terms of the information it can provide and its limitations. Our experiences also strongly indicate that supporting focused educational research represents a different and promising approach to faculty development, one that results in useful institutional outcomes, legitimizes research on instruction as scholarly activity (Boyer, 1990), and has an important and lasting impact on faculty participants' professional lives.

Notes

1. That the seminar is not designed as a how-to-teach-better experience is stressed at the outset. This does not imply, however, that teaching improvement was not an important outcome. Discussions of teaching techniques took place in the context of examining the empirical and theoretical literature. Another seminar at this comprehensive university, The Scholarship of Teaching and Learning, also focuses on student motivation and thinking but does not undertake a comprehensive analysis of the underlying theory or empirical basis for the conclusions or the recommendation for improving student learning. Neither does its content include enhancing faculty research capabilities.

2. Solicitation for participation consisted of announcing to faculty that a new program would provide them with the resources and time to study and to conduct research on teaching and learning. Faculty were informed they would participate in the seminar, review theories and research concerned with how students learn and what motivates students, conduct studies on student thinking and motivation in their own classes or departments, and communicate their results to their colleagues and the university community. They received a one-course teaching reduction during the first year and further support while conducting research.

3. There were twenty-one different disciplines (approximately two-thirds of those in the university) represented in the first three cohorts: accounting, art, biology, communication and theater arts, education, English, foreign languages, geography, industrial technology, interior design, leadership and counseling, mathematics, merchandising, music, nursing, political science, psychology, special education, teacher education, social work, and student affairs.

4. Each year a new cohort is selected for participation. Thus, at any given time, there are faculty at various stages of the program, which currently supports from fifteen to twenty faculty annually.

References

Ames, C. "Achievement Goals and the Classroom Motivational Climate." In D. H. Schunk and J. L. Meece (eds.), *Student Perceptions in the Classroom.* Hillsdale, N.J.: Erlbaum, 1992.
Angelo, T. A., and Cross, K. P. *Classroom Assessment Techniques: A Handbook for College Teachers.* (2nd ed.) San Francisco: Jossey-Bass, 1993.
Bandura, A. "Self-Efficacy Mechanism in Human Agency." *American Psychologist,* 1982, *37,* 122–147.
Boyer, E. *Scholarship Reconsidered: Priorities of the Professoriate.* Princeton, N.J.: Carnegie Foundation for the Advancement of Teaching, 1990.
Brickman, P. "Models of Helping and Coping." *American Psychologist,* 1982, *37,* 368–384.
Cashin, B., and Clegg, V. L. *Periodicals Related to College Teaching.* Manhattan: Kansas State University Center for Faculty Evaluation & Development, 1993.
Collins-Eaglin, J., and Karabenick, S. A. "Motivation in College Classes: Are Goal Orientations

and Incentive Structures Likely to Facilitate or Impede Academic Performance?" Paper presented at the Annual Meeting of the American Educational Research Association, New Orleans, Apr. 1994.

Donald, J. G. "Knowledge Structures: Methods for Exploring Course Content." *Journal of Higher Education,* 1983, *54,* 31–41.

Donald, J. G. "University Professors' Views of Knowledge and Validation Processes." *Journal of Educational Psychology,* 1990, *82,* 242–249.

Johnson, G. R., Eison, J. A., Abbott, R., Guy, T. M., Moran, K., Gorgan, J. A., Pasternack, T. L., Zaremba, E., and McKeachie, W. J. *Teaching Tips for Users of the Motivated Strategies for Learning Questionnaire.* Ann Arbor: University of Michigan, National Center for Research to Improve Postsecondary Teaching and Learning, 1991.

Karabenick, S. A., and Collins-Eaglin, J. "Student Learning in Higher Education: Whose Responsibility Is It?" Paper presented at the Annual Meeting of the American Educational Research Association, San Francisco, Apr. 1995.

Karabenick, S. A., and Knapp, J. R. "Relationship of Academic Help Seeking to the Use of Learning Strategies and other Instrumental Achievement Behavior in College Students." *Journal of Educational Psychology,* 1991, *83,* 221–230.

Karabenick, S. A., and Sharma, R. "Perceived Teacher Support of Student Questioning in the College Classroom: Its Relation to Student Characteristics and Role in the Classroom Questioning Process." *Journal of Educational Psychology,* 1994, *86,* 90–103.

Light, J. "Harvard Seminar on Assessment: Final Report." Cambridge, Mass.: Harvard University, Graduate School of Education, 1990.

Light, J. "Harvard Seminar on Assessment: Final Report." Cambridge, Mass.: Harvard University, Graduate School of Education, 1992.

Light, J., Singer, J. D., and Willett, J. B. *By Design: Planning Research on Higher Education.* Cambridge, Mass.: Harvard University Press, 1990.

McCombs, B. L. "Motivational Skills Training: Combining Metacognitive, Cognitive, and Affective Learning Strategies." In C. E. Weinstein, E. T. Goetz, and P. A. Alexander (eds.), *Learning and Study Strategies: Issues in Assessment, Instruction, and Evaluation.* San Diego: Academic Press, 1988.

McKeachie, W. J. "Research on College Teaching: The Historical Background." *Journal of Educational Psychology,* 1990, *82,* 189–200.

McKeachie, W. J., Pintrich, P. R., Lin, Y.-G., Smith, D.A.F., and Sharma, R. *Teaching and Learning in the College Classroom: A Review of the Research Literature.* Ann Arbor: University of Michigan, National Center for Research to Improve Postsecondary Teaching and Learning, 1990.

Marshall, C., and Rossman, G. B. *Designing Qualitative Research.* Newbury Park, Calif.: Sage, 1989.

Naveh-Benjamin, M., and Lin, Y.-G. "The Effects of Explicitly Teaching an Instructor's Knowledge Structure on Students' Cognitive Structures." Paper presented at the American Psychological Association convention, Atlanta, Apr. 1988.

Naveh-Benjamin, M., and Lin, Y.-G. "Assessing the Flexibility of Cognitive Structures Created in University Courses." Paper presented at the American Psychological Association convention, New Orleans, Apr. 1989.

Naveh-Benjamin, M., and Lin, Y.-G. *Assessing Students' Organization of Concepts: A Manual for Measuring Course-Specific Knowledge Structures.* Ann Arbor: University of Michigan, National Center for Research to Improve Postsecondary Teaching and Learning, 1991.

Naveh-Benjamin, M., McKeachie, W. J., Lin, Y.-G., and Tucker, D. G. "Inferring Students' Cognitive Structures and Their Development Using the 'Ordered Tree Technique.'" *Journal of Educational Psychology,* 1986, *78,* 130–140.

Newman, R. S. "Goals and Self-Regulated Learning: What Motivates Children to Seek Academic Help?" In M. L. Maehr and P. R. Pintrich (eds.), *Advances in Motivation and Achievement.* Vol. 7: *Goals and Self-Regulatory Processes.* Greenwich, Conn.: JAI Press, 1991.

Patton, M. Q. *How to Use Qualitative Methods in Evaluation*. Newbury Park, Calif.: Sage, 1987.

Pintrich, P. R., Smith, D.A.F., Garcia, T., and McKeachie, W. J. "Reliability and Predictive Validity of the Motivated Strategies for Learning Questionnaire (MSLQ)." *Educational and Psychological Measurement*, 1993, *53*, 801–813.

Pittenger, D. J. "The Utility of the Myers-Briggs Type Indicator." *Review of Educational Research*, 1993, *63*, 467–488.

Reitman, J. S., and Reuter, H. H. "Organization Revealed by Recall Orders and Confirmed by Pauses." *Cognitive Psychology*, 1980, *12*, 554–581.

Schmeck, R. R. "Individual Differences in Learning Strategies." In C. E. Weinstein, E. T. Goetz, and P. A. Alexander (eds.), *Learning and Study Strategies: Issues in Assessment, Instruction, and Evaluation*. San Diego: Academic Press, 1988.

Slavin, R. E. "When Does Cooperative Learning Increase Student Achievement?" *Psychological Bulletin*, 1983, *94*, 429–445.

Slavin, R. E., Sharan, S., Kagan, S., Hertz-Lazarowitz, R., Webb, C., and Schmuck, R. (eds.), *Learning to Cooperate, Cooperating to Learn*. New York: Plenum, 1985.

Tobias, S. "Interest, Prior Knowledge, and Learning." *Review of Educational Research*, 1994, *64*, 37–54.

Weimer, M. *Improving College Teaching: Strategies for Developing Instructional Effectiveness*. San Francisco: Jossey-Bass, 1990.

Weiner, B. "A Theory of Motivation for Some Classroom Experiences." *Journal of Educational Psychology*, 1979, *71*, 3–25.

Weiner, B. *An Attributional Theory of Motivation and Emotion*. New York: Springer-Verlag, 1986.

Weinstein, C. E., and Mayer, R. E. "The Teaching of Learning Strategies." In M. C. Wittrock (ed.), *Handbook of Research on Teaching*. (3rd ed.) New York: Macmillan, 1986.

Weinstein, C. E., Palmer, D. R., and Schulte, A. C. *Learning and Study Strategies Inventory*. Clearwater, Fla.: H & H, 1987.

Weinstein, C. E., Zimmerman, S. A., and Palmer, D. R. "Assessing Learning Strategies: The Design and Development of the LASSI." In C. E. Weinstein, E. T. Goetz, and P. A. Alexander (eds.), *Learning and Study Strategies: Issues in Assessment, Instruction, and Evaluation*. San Diego: Academic Press, 1988.

Wittrock, M. "Students' Thought Processes." In M. C. Wittrock (ed.), *Handbook of Research on Teaching*. (3rd ed.) New York: Macmillan, 1986.

STUART A. KARABENICK *is professor of psychology, director of the Center for Research Support, and codirector of the Research on Teaching and Learning program at Eastern Michigan University.*

JAN COLLINS-EAGLIN *is assistant professor of teacher education and codirector of the Research on Teaching and Learning program at Eastern Michigan University.*

*The instructor of an organic chemistry course describes in detail how
he has used ideas about student motivation and self-regulated learning
to change chemistry instruction at his university.*

Progress in Practice: Using Concepts from Motivational and Self-Regulated Learning Research to Improve Chemistry Instruction

Brian P. Coppola

The tradition of active public discourse on chemistry teaching and learning began with the first contribution to the first issue of the *Journal of Chemical Education* (Cornog and Colbert, 1924). National and international meetings devoted to chemistry education have been held for nearly thirty years, and the first Gordon Research Conference on chemistry education was held in 1994. Very early in my experience as an organic chemistry instructor, I was drawn to a single phrase that made me believe that scientists other than chemists could have something to say about chemistry instruction and learning: "cognitive process instruction" (Lochhead and Clement, 1979). Since then, my classroom has been a crucible in which I have fused my knowledge of chemistry with the learning I have done in collaboration with researchers in education and psychology. Although there are other such individual efforts to bridge the gap between places in the university that are linked by their mutual interest in instruction, departments and schools of psychology and education remain fundamentally isolated from chemistry and the other arts, humanities, and sciences.

In this chapter, I report on how students in my content-filled subject matter course in introductory organic chemistry (called Structure and Reactivity) have benefited from their instructor's ability to recognize, translate, and contextualize notions from motivation and self-regulated learning; and I discuss a number of strategies that I use in my chemistry courses.

General Guiding Principles of Instruction

Four principles have guided my thinking as I have made changes in my instructional methods.

1. *Give out the implicit rules.* Every discipline creates linguistic and symbolic representations for concepts in order to facilitate communication. In professional associations, we share critical assumptions about representations and rules of operation used by our disciplines, including how these are connected to one other. Beginning learners in any area strive to build a picture based on necessarily incomplete information, and their understanding lacks the sophistication that allows experts to make judgments based on information that is only implied and not at all apparent in the surface features of any word, symbol, or action. The strategies outlined here all provide a way for students and faculty to check the progress of students' learning.

2. *Use Socratic instruction.* Anything that turns a passive listener into an active participant is a good thing. Unlike others who advocate dismantling the lecture classroom, I claim that what you do with your class time is the key. Certainly, a lecture to a group of novice learners cannot be like a professional seminar because the audience lacks all of the prior knowledge and shared assumptions and understandings of a professional group. However, it may not be necessary to demand individual accountability on the part of every student when a question is asked (as is the benefit in small-group work) but rather to give each student the opportunity to respond out loud to questions along with hundreds of others. I regularly teach in a 400-seat lecture hall. I do not need to hear every answer as I count to ten after asking a question, but instead, I want all of my students to understand that I want them thinking in their seats about the hour's topics and that I intend for all of them to participate. Some instructors make the error of only acknowledging the expected response among the noisy clamor, affirming the efforts of those who "got it right" without considering how and why other attentive learners could come to the "wrong" answer. I explore the range of possible solutions that students offer. That allows me to demonstrate the kind of reasoning skills I want the students to emulate. If I trust that the unexpected answer has been arrived at by some deliberate process, then I must deconstruct the argument to make the logical error appear; simply stating the correctness of an answer is always the easiest thing to do and the most comfortable for students who willingly accede authority, but it is the least constructive for learning. Another possibility among students who have very limited amounts of knowledge to draw from is that the "incorrect" answer is really quite reasonable and internally consistent with what they know at the time. Depending on the specific situation, I will either acknowledge the correctness of that conclusion as consistent within reasonable expectation, or I will use it as an opportunity to present new information. I ask open questions nearly every time I judge that I am making an informed decision, which makes the questions very brief, concrete, and focused rather than broadly philosophical. The opportunities to ask questions arise sponta-

neously, so they might occur three times in one minute or after a ten-minute monologue, but the effect is a kind of conversation between me and the class.

3. *Create alternative metaphors for learning.* When we instructors say "study, learn, and do problems," we do not account for the variety of strategies students have for studying, learning, and doing problems. I might memorize and recite lists of items as one way to learn if I judge that to be an appropriate strategy. But as an expert learner, I have developed a toolbox of techniques, and I readily create new tools as I need them, refining and discarding them according to the tenets of self-regulation. What do we mean when we say, "Do problems"? How can I express the difference to students who beat on every problem they face with the same wooden club, and who might easily look at one of my sophisticated, refined tools; pick it up; and start to hammer away with it too? One strategy is to use metaphor.

4. *Make examinations reflect course goals.* A set of examinations outlines the expectations, or goals, of a course much better than a syllabus. If these goals also include higher-order learning and thinking skills, then care must be taken to actively preclude unwanted skills. In other words, if I do not want memorization and recitation to be successful, then I must design tasks that do not reinforce these skills, and I must include explicit instruction for alternative strategies.

Specific Strategies for Active and Socratic Learning and Instruction

I use or suggest the following strategies very often because they are the kinds of skills I want my students to see me demonstrating and discussing in the context of the subject matter and that I want them to develop as habits as they learn.

Cognitive Modeling, or, Thinking Out Loud. I want to extend instruction from delivering knowledge alone to including how knowledge is created and used. This requires a great deal of reflection and introspection, as our own understanding of the most basic features of our disciplines is most often not explicit but rather a set of tacit assumptions shared by the professional community. This type of modeling by instructors helps students see others' risking, become metacognitively aware of their own ways of creating and using knowledge, and one hopes, begin to regulate their own thinking. I want students to see me take inventory of factual information, account for its limitations, and then draw meaning from the implications against the backdrop of my prior knowledge. Gorrell (1993) describes the advantage of providing implicit rules within a framework of cognitive modeling. One skill that students have rarely developed is the ability to suspend judgment while many possible interpretations are checked against the context of all given information. My students have a very strong need for one-to-one, logically dependent relationships: "Whenever I see 'H_3O^+' as a chemical reagent, what should I write as an answer?" The unsatisfying response, "It depends," describes how we rely on the context: what else is around, what are the typical behaviors, and under what conditions do they occur? Students are uncomfortable with the uncertainty of science. How experts balance all of the information presented in a given situation needs to be explicitly modeled and reflected upon. The interpretation of spectroscopic data is another good example of a topic where a great deal of experience and unrepresented information needs to be unpacked in order to translate the lines and squiggles of a graphic output into an interpretation.

Using Analogies. Analogies are one of the most powerful tools we use in understanding. Analogies presume the interconnected nature of knowledge, because we seek to make the unfamiliar comprehensible in terms of a relationship to our prior knowledge. The habit of creating analogies stands out as the most identifiable outcome of my own graduate training. Whether I encounter a new chemical reaction described in a chemistry journal or an unfamiliar notion in educational psychology, my instinct is to presuppose a connection to something I know and to wonder out loud, "What is this like?" For students, analogies can fulfill two roles. At the beginning of a course, they can connect new concepts from an unfamiliar discipline to students' previous experience ("When the two molecules collide, three of the groups attached to the carbon atom unfold and invert like an umbrella in the wind"). Later in the course, lateral connections can be made by grouping similar ideas together ("When they undergo collisions, the atoms in the following set all behave like the carbon atoms you have learned about already"). Another common verbal exchange in my class starts with this question: "If I use [this]$_a$ as an analogy, what do I expect? And if I use [this]$_b$ as an analogy, what now?" After exploring the logical consistency of the responses, I discuss how to decide which analogy is most appropriate, after which the design of experiments to test alternative interpretations becomes meaningful.

Using Counterintuitive Examples. I understood the value of counterintuitive examples in a Socratic environment the first time 300 students all yelled out, with great confidence, the "wrong" answer. These situations occur when students use uninformed models to make decisions. The counterintuitive example is really nothing more than the usual laboratory observation of an "unexpected result." For example, a common correlation discussed in introductory chemistry is that of the observed hydrogen ion acidities for bonds derived from atoms within the same row of the periodic table with the trend in the property known as electronegativity. In chemistry, there is a great tendency to use causal language ("the trend in acidity is *due to* electronegativity") rather than correlative language ("the trend in acidity is correlated with electronegativity"). Students, who seem to prefer simple, universal models, will extrapolate this causal language to all acidity relationships. So when students are asked to predict the relative acidities of similar molecules made up of atoms from a column of the periodic table, they use the electronegativity model easily, consistently, confidently, and vocally. This is an appropriate example of making an analogy, after all. Unfortunately, the experimental result in this case is just the opposite from the prediction. That does not make the prediction wrong, because the model is being used correctly. It is simply a reflection of scientific practice according to Thomas Henry Huxley: beautiful theories are killed by ugly facts. Although there is a danger that some will become relativists, many students seem to learn from these examples how and when people need to increase the factors to which they attribute phenomena. After a few rounds of examples such as this one, applied liberally at the beginning of the course, the class starts to develop a healthy skepticism about my questions. I am exhorted to "give out the experimental result," or I might get more conditional answers: "If it turns out this way, then this factor must be more responsible than that one. . . . If it turns out the other way, then . . ."

Providing Heuristics. Providing heuristics is an aspect of cognitive modeling that deserves its own mention. In every subject, we have personally meaningful learning tools or strategies that allow us to make decisions or recall information and relationships more easily. In organic chemistry, one of these tools might be the way I decide which of six outcomes from four possible reaction pathways might be expected to occur. Concept maps can help the instructor and the student represent such information and externalize the ideas for better discussion (Novak and Gowin, 1984; Markham, Mintzes, and Jones, 1994; Nakhleh, 1994; Pendley, Bretz, and Novak, 1994). Mnemonics are another useful tool (Fieser and Fieser, 1956, p. 359; Williams, 1992).

Changing Teacher/Student Roles. One of the most startling revelations for my students occurs when they realize that our roles explicitly reverse during an examination. As the questioner, I am now going to them for advice on how to solve a problem. For those ninety minutes, they need to see themselves in the role of the instructor, to engage in the kinds of behaviors they would while working with their friends or study group partners rather than to think of themselves as the repository of prescribed answers. Examinations are to be engaged actively, and by having the reversal of roles pointed out to them, students can appreciate the value of working with others before an exam. One way or the other, we instructors demand *performance* on an exam, and the worst time to consider the ins and outs of articulation for the first time is during the exam itself.

Using New Metaphors for Teaching and Learning. Students need help in understanding the role metaphors play in shaping disciplines and how metaphors can help them in their own learning.

The Narrative of Science. The concept that all disciplines are sophisticated narratives created by humans is not appreciated very well by students. The rhetoric of moving naïve objectivist notions to more constructivist epistemologies currently occupies a central position in science education research (Garafalo and LoPresti, 1993; Roth, 1993). Careful attention to language in our classes can, I believe, help students understand these ideas. I never miss the opportunity to use the expression "telling a story" when I provide chemistry's rationalizations for phenomena. To support this viewpoint, I bring in quotes from external sources, including the article title "Telling the Stories of

Educational Psychology" (Berliner, 1992) and the following observation by Ackroyd (1989): "Science is like fiction, you see. We make up stories, we sketch out narratives, we try to find some pattern beneath events. We are interested observers. And we like to go on with the story, we like to advance, we like to make progress. Even though they are stories told in the dark" (p. 159). On occasion, at the beginning and then at the end of the year, I have asked my students to complete the following assertion: "Chemistry is a science where . . ." At the beginning of the year, in general and overwhelmingly, students write: "Chemistry is a science where atoms and molecules are studied." By the end of the year, nearly all of the responses carry interesting and sometimes profound perspectives: "Atoms and molecules may be the building blocks of matter, but there is no cohesion, that is, the 'big picture,' without chemistry."

The Performance Studio. Most instructors encourage students to work with each other for a variety of reasons, but the common thread that runs through these rationales is the same: you really learn the material when you have to teach it. I assert that a broader reason is imbedded here, one that comes very naturally to disciplines such as art, theater, and dance in which *performance* is explicitly recognized as the way individuals regulate their learning. In these disciplines, we understand the role of performance as we learn, and our perspective on learning is always cognizant of our need to share what we have learned with others. Evaluating task performance is at the heart of examinations. I further assert that learners who take their need to articulate into account, by whatever method is required by the context, are doing more than just enacting their skills, they are also anticipating the teaching aspect of their learning. Learning to solve chemistry problems, then, is metaphorically related to the studio time required in an art or music class. This is a notion that can be easily shared with and understood by students.

The Persistent Learner. Persistence is a key outcome of motivated learning. One belief that I want to support is the idea that learners always construct their understanding by seeking and creating larger patterns (the "big picture"), by grouping, ungrouping, and regrouping the interconnected individual ideas. There is a great deal of intellectual risk, at the cost of ego, in backing away from a perceived pattern, even if all of the pieces do not quite fit. (What is even worse is to believe that you are simply not capable of seeing any pattern at all because of a fundamental inadequacy. Then there might be a conscious decision to not invest the energy to persist, and that is a different situation.) But I have observed very capable students who seem to lack the awareness that they must actively move back and forth between smaller and larger concepts, constantly checking and rechecking the internal consistency of the picture they are constructing.

Using Texts in a Self-Regulated Manner. My experience with chemistry students and textbooks is discouraging. I have asked students to describe their textbook habits many times, and the majority of them read their texts as they might a novel, in a linear deliberate march that presupposes that every nuance on page 251 needs to be assimilated before they go on to page 252. Not surprisingly, the contextualized problems within a chapter are always "easier" than the uncontextualized ones at the end of the chapter, and a significant number of students simply treat the worked-out answers for the latter in the answer manuals as another kind of text, to look at, outline, and highlight. Alternative strategies for using textbooks can be suggested. Here are two examples:

First, tell students to "sketch out" their understanding by concentrating on what they can understand as a starting point. I remind students to treat chapters as whole units, and I recommend multiple cursory passes through the information in order to get a feel for the broad context and to look for repetition in the discussion. As in painting a portrait, it is a bad idea to articulate any one feature with too much detail too early—the perspective and proportion of the whole picture will tend to distort around that feature. Instead, painters first sketch and then incrementally refine, always with an eye on relationships between details and the whole.

Second, tell students to "separate reading time from problem time and think about starting with the problems." By starting with the problems, a student can begin to make discriminations about the information in a text. But this does not mean searching for the appropriate pages to solve the problem; it is, rather, just getting a sense of the ideas. Linking a problem with the reading about it creates a context, but is not a very useful skill to take into an exam. Students need to be explicitly reminded of the value of learning that they do not yet have enough information to categorize or solve a problem. They need to know that an important way to gauge their level of understanding is to admit what they can and cannot do. This type of textbook learning is much more in line with a self-regulated learning approach to reading texts than is the linear and deliberate type.

Changing Exam and Grading Policies. When those of us teaching chemistry examined how to achieve departmental goals in the introductory organic chemistry course, we recognized that organic chemistry was structured in such a way that state-of-the-art information, derived from the primary literature, could be presented to novice students on their examinations. This strategy assures us that we are being honest to the actual facts of science and not simply inventing trivial derivatives of classroom examples. Each citation from the primary literature is accompanied by some contextualizing statements. The citations send two messages to the students: first, that just memorizing all of the textbook examples is not enough and, second, that understanding the subject matter of the introductory course allows them to understand some of what chemists actually say about the things they study. The contexts of these problems carry a great deal of intrinsic interest, or relevancy, because many of the examples come from the areas of medicinal and pharmaceutical chemistry or materials science. In a sense, the examination questions I use are like short case studies.

I also reinforce the idea of multiple representations for the same phenomenon. A student might be asked to provide word, picture, and numerical versions of the same idea. There are many times when there are four, five, or more correct solutions within the context of the course and the information provided in a question. On nearly every exam, students suggest completely reasonable alternative solutions that I did not anticipate. These are also important lessons for instructors to make note of as they teach their classes.

Finally, because students develop their new skills at different rates and because the course is truly cumulative each step along the way, those of us teaching chemistry have devised ways to make improvement count. One simple but effective technique is increasing the point value of exams throughout the term without increasing the length of the exam. It is "worth" more to do better later, so students do not feel they have to be perfect at the outset, and their practice has tangible value for them. I also make judgments about improvement by considering the set of exams and the final as two independent measures of cumulative performance. Herschbach (1993) keeps an account of the points lost during the term as a function of topic. Students who master these topics on the final have their earlier points "resurrected" in an accounting of their grade.

Conclusion

Education is not a neutral activity, and it is a collaborative process. As instructors, we all are changing the way our students think about the world, and we are interested in assisting the change in a productive way. We can learn a great deal by listening and watching our students carefully as they learn. At the outset, instructors should establish an explicit and common agenda of instructional goals with their students, so that everyone is working toward the same end. Otherwise, the intrinsic cognitive dissonance will always put instructors and students at crossed purposes.

I have spent over ten years grappling with the implications of what psychology and education have to say about instruction and learning. I have discovered that ideas from motivation and self-regulated learning can play a significant role in the instructional design of real classrooms comprising hundreds of students taking introductory chemistry. The development of ideas needs to flow in both directions: between the pedagogical content knowledge of the instructor as an expert in his or her field and the theoretical constructs of education and learning research.

The implementation of the strategies I describe here has been integral to the structure of the course. As one of my students remarked last year, "You know what's nice about this course? Not only is it obvious that you have an instructional plan, but you have also let us in on it." From my viewpoint, three lessons from my experience with the design and implementation of the introductory organic chemistry course stand out.

First, instruction that encourages students to develop higher-order skills is best accomplished within a well-defined discipline from which the contextualized expertise of faculty can be drawn. I am a trained organic chemist, and the pedagogical content knowledge (Clermont, Borko, and Krajcik, 1994) I bring to this course allows me to construct the most meaningful kind of learning environment for my students. The notions of "anchored," or "situated," learning ring true and argue against the general survey course (Brown, Collins, and Duguid, 1989; The Cognition and Technology Group at Vanderbilt, 1990, 1992; Lave and Wenger, 1991). In addition, my experience shows that ideas about motivation and self-regulated learning can be used in a content-filled class. They do not have to be used only in generic learning and thinking skills classes.

Second, new faculty can adapt to very different instructional environments than the ones they have known and contribute in positive, creative ways if a system of education and support is created. In many ways, the same techniques instructors use to make instructional goals and strategies explicit for their students can be used to engage faculty.

Third, the concept of collaboration across the university in order to advance instruction and learning makes sense. I am sure that our students who report that they "certainly learned more than chemistry" are reflecting the practical benefits of theoretically sound design. My colleagues in chemistry, psychology, and education are actively pursuing these leads with me.

References

Ackroyd, P. *First Light.* New York: Grove Weidenfeld, 1989.

Berliner, D. C. "Telling the Stories of Educational Psychology." *Educational Psychologist,* 1992, 27 (2), 143–161.

Brown, J. S., Collins, A., and Duguid, P. "Situated Cognition and the Culture of Learning." *Educational Researcher,* 1989, 18 (1), 32–42.

Clermont, C. P., Borko, H., and Krajcik, J. S. "Comparative Study of the Pedagogical Content Knowledge of Experienced and Novice Chemical Demonstrators." *Journal of Research in Science Teaching,* 1994, 31 (4), 419–441.

The Cognition and Technology Group at Vanderbilt. "Anchored Instruction and Its Relationship to Situated Cognition." *Educational Researcher,* 1990, 19 (5), 2–10.

The Cognition and Technology Group at Vanderbilt. "The Jasper Series and an Example of Anchored Instruction: Theory, Program, Description, and Assessment Data." *Educational Psychologist,* 1992, 17 (3), 291–315.

Cornog, J., and Colbert, J. C. "What We Teach Our Freshman in Chemistry." *Journal of Chemical Education,* 1924, 1 (1), 5–12.

Fieser, L. F., and Fieser, M. *Organic Chemistry.* (3rd ed.) New York: Reinhold, 1956.

Garafalo, F., and LoPresti, V. "Evolution of an Integrated College Freshman Curriculum: Using Educational Research Findings as a Guide." *Journal of Chemical Education,* 1993, 70 (5), 352–359.

Gorrell, J. "Cognitive Modeling and Implicit Rules: Effects on Problem-Solving Performance." *American Journal of Psychology,* 1993, 106 (1), 51–65.

Herschbach, D. R. "Paradigms in Research and Parables in Teaching." *Journal of Chemical Education,* 1993, 70 (5), 391–392.

Lave, J., and Wenger, E. *Situated Learning: Legitimate Peripheral Participation.* Cambridge, England: Cambridge University Press, 1991.

Lochhead, J., and Clement, J. (eds.). *Cognitive Process Instruction.* Philadelphia: Franklin Institute Press, 1979.

Markham, K. M., Mintzes, J. J., and Jones, M. G. "The Concept Map as a Research and Evaluation Tool: Further Evidence of Validity." *Journal of Research in Science Teaching,* 1994, 31 (1), 91–101.

Nakhleh, M. B. "Chemical Education Research in the Laboratory Environment." *Journal of Chemical Education,* 1994, *71* (3), 201–205.

Novak, J. D., and Gowin, D. B. *Learning How to Learn.* Cambridge, England: Cambridge University Press, 1984.

Pendley, B. D., Bretz, R. L., and Novak, J. D. "Concept Maps as a Tool to Assess Learning in Chemistry." *Journal of Chemical Education,* 1994, *71* (1), 9–15.

Roth, W.-M. "In the Name of Constructivism: Science Education Research and the Construction of Local Knowledge." *Journal of Research in Science Teaching,* 1993, *30* (7), 799–803.

Williams, J. P. "A Mnemonic for the Krebs Cycle." *Journal of Chemical Education,* 1992, *69* (12), 985–986.

BRIAN P. COPPOLA is lecturer in chemistry and coordinator for undergraduate organic chemistry curriculum at the University of Michigan, Ann Arbor.

INDEX

Achievement: and classroom context, 48–50; and cognitive strategies, 74; and competitiveness, 50–51; and defensive pessimism, 33; and psychological distress, 78; and self-efficacy, 45–46; and self-handicapping, 33

Achievement goals. *See* Goals; Mastery goals; Performance goals

Ackroyd, P., 92

Alkin, M. C., 58

American Association of Community Colleges, 57

Ames, C., 7, 43, 46, 48, 51, 76

Angelo, T. A., 72

Archer, J., 48, 49

Assessment: and Motivated Strategies for Learning Questionnaire, 76; and Learning and Study Strategies Inventory, 76; of learning, 9; for motivation/learning strategies, 9

Attention: and motivational control, 65–66; and self-monitoring, 64–65

Bandura, A., 6, 10, 14, 15, 16, 17, 18, 19, 46, 49, 53, 59, 60, 76

Baumeister, R. F., 31, 32

Behavior: and goal structure, 48; and learning, 5, 7; student, and learning (example), 5–7; student awareness of, 9

Berglas, S., 21

Berliner, D. C., 92

Blumenfield, P. C., 46

Borko, H., 94

Borokowski, J. G., 59, 68

Boyer, E., 72, 80, 83

Bradley, L., 21, 22

Bretz, R. L., 91

Brickman, P., 78

Brown, J. S., 95

Byrnes, J. P., 18

Cantor, N., 30, 32, 40

Carstens, C. B., 18

Carver, C. S., 16

Cashin, B., 77

Chemistry instruction: and analogic examples, 90; and cognitive modeling, 89–90; and counter-intuitive examples, 90–91; and exam/grading policies, 93–94; guiding principles of, 88–89; and heuristics, 91; and narrative of science, 91–92; new metaphors for, 91–92; and persistent learner, 92; and performance studio, 92; and teacher/student roles, 91; and textbooks, 92–93. *See also* Teaching

Classroom assessment techniques (CATs), 72, 73

Classroom context, and achievement motivation/goals, 48–50

Classroom research, 72. *See also* Discipline-focused educational research program

Clegg, V. L., 77

Clement, J., 87

Clermont, C. P., 94

Cognition: and discipline-focused educational research program, 74; and learning, 5, 7; student, and learning (example), 5–7; student awareness of, 9. *See also* Cognitive strategies

Cognition and Technology Group at Vanderbilt, The, 95

Cognitive strategies: and achievement, 74; control of, 7; defined, 74; feedback on, 9; and test taking, 7; and thinking out loud, 89–90; and volition, 59. *See also* Cognition; Learning strategies

Colbert, J. C., 87

Cole, M., 67

Colleges/universities, and self-regulated learning, 8–9. *See also* Community colleges

Collins, A., 95

Collins, K. W., 60, 65

Collins-Eaglin, J., 77

Community colleges: diversity in, 57; students of, 57–58; volitional enhancement program for, 60–69. *See also* Colleges/universities

Competition: and achievement, 50–51; vs. individualism, 48, 52

Corno, L., 14, 58, 59, 60

Cornog, J., 87

Covington, M. V., 6, 29, 31, 32, 40, 58

Cross, K. P., 58, 72

ORDERING INFORMATION

NEW DIRECTIONS FOR TEACHING AND LEARNING is a series of paperback books that presents ideas and techniques for improving college teaching, based both on the practical expertise of seasoned instructors and on the latest research findings of educational and psychological researchers. Books in the series are published quarterly in spring, summer, fall, and winter and are available for purchase by subscription as well as by single copy.

SUBSCRIPTIONS for 1995 cost $48.00 for individuals (a savings of 25 percent over single-copy prices) and $64.00 for institutions, agencies, and libraries. Please do not send institutional checks for personal subscriptions. Standing orders are accepted. (For subscriptions outside of North America, add $7.00 for shipping via surface mail or $25.00 for air mail. Orders *must be prepaid* in U.S. dollars by check drawn on a U.S. bank or charged to VISA, MasterCard, or American Express.)

SINGLE COPIES cost $16.95 plus shipping (see below) when payment accompanies order. California, New Jersey, New York, and Washington, D.C., residents please include appropriate sales tax. Canadian residents add GST and any local taxes. Billed orders will be charged shipping and handling. No billed shipments to post office boxes. (Orders from outside North America *must be prepaid* in U.S. dollars by check drawn on a U.S. bank or charged to VISA, MasterCard, or American Express.)

SHIPPING (SINGLE COPIES ONLY): one issue, add $3.50; two issues, add $4.50; three to four issues, add $5.50; five issues, add $6.50; six to eight issues, add $7.50; nine or more issues, add $8.50.

DISCOUNTS FOR QUANTITY ORDERS are available. Please write to the address below for information.

ALL ORDERS must include either the name of an individual or an official purchase order number. Please submit your order as follows:
    Subscriptions: specify series and year subscription is to begin
    Single copies: include individual title code (such as TL54)

MAIL ALL ORDERS TO:
    Jossey-Bass Publishers
    350 Sansome Street
    San Francisco, CA 94104-1342

FOR SUBSCRIPTION SALES OUTSIDE OF THE UNITED STATES, CONTACT:
    any international subscription agency or Jossey-Bass directly.